Overcoming the Odds

How I won £50,000 of prizes in three years

REBECCA BEESLEY

THANK YOU

Thank you for purchasing this book.
All profits from the sale of this book will go to Juvenile Arthritis Research in the search for a cure for juvenile idiopathic arthritis.

For more information, see www.jarproject.org.

DEDICATION

To my three totally awesome kids who
inspire me every single day …

Joshua, Daniel and Trinity.

CONTENTS

ACKNOWLEDGMENTS

@mustardbomb – aka Neill. I think of Neill as my very best comping friend. Since I came across his blog http://luckmuscle.blogspot.com a few years ago I kept coming back to read it time and time again. I loved that Neill writes about the ups, downs, fun and frustrations of comping with such honesty. When I asked Neill whether he'd be able to give this book a quick read through I had no idea just what an amazing job he would do. He did an epic editing job that I am forever grateful for. He once used the analogy of being like a midwife for this book and I can't think of a better midwife to have had to help give birth to this book. Thank you.

@superluckydi – aka Di Coke. Anyone familiar with competitions will know that Di is an absolute comping legend. I know my own comping hobby stepped up to another level when I came across Di and her Superlucky blog and Facebook page. This wonderful lady is passionate about sharing this hobby with others and giving them all the know-how to get started. She advises promoters and brands on best practice when it comes to running competitions and inspires compers all around the world! It is an understatement to say that it is an honour to have Di write the foreword for this book. I am truly grateful.

I've listed Instagram handles above for these awesome people who have helped make this book what it is. Do give them a follow and be prepared to be inspired.

Thank you to Tom Horner at The Upper Room who stepped in at very short notice to create a book cover for *Overcoming the Odds*. Thank you, Tom, for your talent and skills in bringing together my very vague idea into a fantastic-looking book cover.

FOREWORD

I first connected with Rebecca back in 2012, when we started enthusiastically emailing each other about comping. We shared a love of blogging and creative competitions, and would discuss the latest fun children's comps we'd discovered! She'd just started her blog, The Beesley Buzz, which has grown to be a wonderful resource of family stories and advice - particularly about juvenile arthritis, which is of course the motivation behind her writing this book.

I try to feature as many winning stories as I can on my blog SuperLucky, and I never tire of reading them. Many people are naturally cynical about comping, and with a large audience I'm in a good position to share stories of real people winning real prizes, demonstrating the joy that comping can bring to your life. I'm always excited to see an email from Rebecca in my inbox as I know it's likely to be another unusual win she wants to tell me about, and I love sharing them at www.superlucky.me!

Rebecca's stories in *Overcoming the Odds* will inspire and entertain you. She has woven comping into her life seamlessly, making it an enjoyable and rewarding hobby for all the family. This book shows what's possible with a little creativity and enthusiasm - and proves that a lack of skill or money should be no barrier to your comping adventures! Rebecca is honest about what it takes to beat the odds and also reminds us to see comping as a fun hobby: if it starts to become an obsession, or no longer enjoyable, then it's fine to take a break.

I hope that *Overcoming the Odds* will intrigue and delight you as much as it did me, and of course that you'll want to give comping a try. Who knows, maybe one day it might be your winning stories featured in a book!

Di Coke (@SuperLuckyDi)
Blogger at www.superlucky.me
Author of *SuperLucky Secrets: 100 tips for winning competitions, contests and sweepstakes*

PREFACE

'This is your life. Be bold with it. Live it with energy and
purpose in the direction that excites you. Listen to your heart,
look for your dreams, they are God-inspired' – Bear Grylls.

This book provides an account of my experiences (and some of my prizes) from my first few years as a 'comper', that is, someone who enjoys entering competitions.

Despite the school holidays, hospital appointments, tantrums and meltdowns (and that was just me!) and the endless procrastination, the pieces have gradually come together.

The final push came when my husband felt a stirring so strong in his heart that he made the possibly crazy but definitely brave decision to quit his job and follow his calling. As with those beautifully powerful words of Bear Grylls quoted here, he decided to quit the grey treadmill of the corporate world, to do something that would make a difference.

He followed his heart and his passion and has set up the JAR Project (www.jarproject.org/support) to search for a cure for juvenile arthritis, a painful autoimmune disorder where the body starts to attack the joints, causing inflammation, pain, discomfort and reduced mobility. Left unchecked, juvenile arthritis can lead to other health conditions as the immune system attacks other organs, as well as permanent disability and long-term health implications.

Our beloved daughter has suffered from juvenile arthritis since she was two, and I have likewise suffered since the age of ten, resulting in my recent total hip replacement surgery at the relatively young age of 40.

At present, there is no cure for juvenile arthritis. All current treatments seek to reduce the symptoms of the disorder, but are not a cure. Whilst these treatments have beneficial effects in reducing pain and inflammation, and provide some protection against long-term joint damage, they come with their own side effects and impinge on the long-term health of children taking these medications. In around half of all cases, children go into spontaneous remission. But in the other half, they are confined to taking powerful drugs long-term, with all the side effects and complications that causes.

This book is my contribution to the JAR Project, as all profits from its sale will go to Juvenile Arthritis Research in the search for a cure for juvenile idiopathic arthritis.

When I first began writing, I had no hope or intention of the book being read beyond my family and perhaps a few friends who have taken an interest in my hobby. But as I write the last few words, it is my hope that it will inspire and encourage others and give them a glimpse of hope at times they need it most.

Comping has given me an escape when things have been tough. It's given me friendships when I've needed them most. It's given our family experiences and memories at times when we could not have afforded them. It's given the children iPads which I could never have bought for them. It's helped others when our prizes have been shared with them. It's helped people in need at times when the money saved by winning a prize could then be given to someone in need of money at that time. It's a hobby that encourages generosity and community, as there are lots of compers who share their prizes and look out for competitions that might interest their comping friends.

It may not be an active pastime like fishing or creative like crafting or baking, but it *is* a hobby nonetheless – and one where your day can go from mundane to magnificent in a single moment.

It has become my passion, and in the words of Fabienne Frederickson 'The things you are passionate about are not random, they are your calling'. It may not be as noble as trying to heal children, but it has brought much joy and happiness to our lives.

Indeed, in recent years, nothing has excited me more than this life-changing hobby of mine. It's the topic I most love talking about. I love seeing others encouraged and enthused to 'have a go' when they hear my stories. And for those who ask how I do it, this is also written for you.

That said, this isn't a 'how to' book. That already exists in the form of Di Coke's *Superlucky Secrets*, which I thoroughly recommend to anyone starting out with this hobby or wanting to pick up new ideas and improve their comping efforts. This is simply my own little way of sharing my experiences with others who want to know more; those who struggle to believe that real people win prizes, that it is possible to have a family holiday with zero budget or that all that baby paraphernalia on your wishlist really can become yours.

Between May 2012 and May 2015 – the three years that I focused more on my comping hobby – I managed to win in excess of £50,000 worth of prizes. I was comping before this period – and I won some wonderful prizes then too – but that was before I started keeping records. The three-year period covered in this book also includes some bona fide 'money can't buy' prizes, such as afternoon tea with Mary Berry. In such instances, I just recorded the 'basic' monetary value of any physical prizes associated with the competition – in this case, a cookery book and a Kenwood K-mix stand mixer. Despite it being the very best part of the prize, I can't possibly put a monetary value on meeting Mary Berry!

Before we proceed, however, let me make one thing clear: I am no queen of compers!

There are many others out there with more experience of entering competitions – and more experience of winning. There are amazing compers who keep up to date with the latest apps and ever-evolving ways of entering competitions.

This book is simply the story about how I was able to change my life with a hobby I discovered and found that I loved. And the great thing is, there's no reason why you can't do the same!

CHAPTER 1

Years of free holidays

The very first holiday win
We have won so many holidays in recent years that I'm ashamed to say I've lost count!

I remember the first one well – mainly because it was before I started 'comping' in earnest. Times had been financially tough when the kids were young. I'd left my job to become a stay-at-home mum. With two young children so close in age, the cost of childcare meant that I hadn't been able to return to my previous career.

Yet holidays were important to us. I don't mean exotic holidays, jet-setting around the world. Rather, just a short break *anywhere* in order to get some respite from the chores and daily grind and to spend some quality time together.

That particular year, we resorted to selling the few pieces of gold jewellery that my mum had left me when she passed away. Despite the sentimental value it held, I had made the decision that making memories with my children and being able to take them away for a few days was of more value to me. So, I reluctantly sold the gold.

It didn't look much, but the value of gold was at a high and we were pleased that it brought in a couple of hundred pounds. We put that together with what we had managed to save and it was just enough for a mid-week summer break at Shorefields, a holiday site in the New Forest.

We had a wonderful time. The children loved the kids craft clubs and evening entertainment. We enjoyed splashing in the pool. The play areas were great and we fell in love with the kids' club mascots Cybil and Cyril the squirrels.

We stayed in a small lodge and even the smallest problem (like the handle breaking off the frying pan) was speedily resolved with super customer service. And so I was only too happy to fill in the customer feedback questionnaire at the end of our stay to say what a great time we had.

I know what you're thinking – that we paid for this holiday with our own hard-earned cash and so whatever has this got to do with winning a holiday? Well…

The following January, an A4 envelope came through the post from Shorefield. January seems to be the time of year that all holiday companies start to advertise, so I was fully expecting the envelope to contain their brochure.

And yes, as expected, it was a brochure. But there was something else too – a covering letter to say that we'd won a holiday there as our customer feedback survey had been drawn as that year's winner!

We booked our stay for later that year. As we were home-schooling at the time, we went off-peak. There was less in the way of entertainment, and not all the kids clubs were running, but it was a fabulous break nonetheless. The prize was a stay in one of their caravans, which the kids loved because of the added novelty factor. They also got a room each, so they enjoyed having their own space.

So, that was our very first holiday win and it turned out to be the first of many…

Cuddledry and Cornwall

The next holiday win came in my first year of truly getting into comping. It was the year my daughter was born and it was during those sleepless nights of breastfeeding into the early hours and scrolling through Facebook where I would come across many of the competitions I entered.

I remember spotting a competition with Cuddledry – the company that makes the innovative baby towel that you can wear like an apron when getting your baby out the bath. I remember seeing the towel on *Dragons' Den* and thinking just what an amazing product it was, as baby bathing had always been a challenge for us. We'd even ask Granny to bath our eldest when he was first born as we found it so tricky.

The competition required entrants to submit a photo with a 'happy baby' theme. We'd recently taken some lovely photos of Trinity and I had just the photo in mind. It might not have been well-composed, but it captured her infectious laugh just perfectly.

We heard we'd been shortlisted but I didn't feel particularly hopeful. At this point, I was in my early days of comping, so the level of expectation was still pretty low. I was therefore genuinely taken aback to find myself scrolling through my Facebook feed only to see that photo of my daughter staring back at me from the Cuddledry page, announced as the winning entry. It was actually judged by a whole host of professional photographers which made it all the more amazing to have been chosen as the winner.

The prize was a £500 voucher with Farm and Cottage holidays (now called Holiday Cottages). Because our kids were still being home-schooled at this point, we booked our holiday to fall just after the end of the school holidays. The voucher covered the best part of a week's stay in a fabulous farm cottage in Cornwall, which came with an outdoor pool too. We paid just a small amount extra to cover the remaining cost.

Bluestone – A last-minute surprise
Although the Cuddledry competition was the first holiday I'd won since Trinity was born and we booked it for the September of that year when she was nearly six months old, it wasn't actually her first holiday.

Her very first holiday was at the end of August that year when we got an e-mail one Friday telling us we'd won a holiday that following week at Bluestone in Wales and that they'd be expecting us on Monday morning. Talk about short notice!

It was too good an opportunity to miss as we worked out that a Monday to Friday break at that time of year, staying in the amazing lodge that had been booked for us, would ordinarily have cost in excess of £1,000.

We'd submitted a family photo via their Facebook page some time ago and it turned out that we'd been picked as one of the families they wanted to use in a photoshoot which would then be potentially used in future publicity. One of the days would be devoted to the photoshoot with a professional photographer and a member of their marketing team, and the remaining days were ours to do as we wished.

On photoshoot day, the boys got to do the climbing wall and mini-jeep driving experience, while we got driven around in the golf buggy – all activities that would normally count as extras. We were also treated to lunch at the Knight's Tafern.

Sadly, despite being promised a copy of the photos, we never did get to see any of them. But despite this (and the wet weather!) the actual break was wonderful. The lodge where we were staying was massive and could accommodate eight people, so we really enjoyed all the space – especially as it was furnished to such a high standard. We were thoroughly impressed.

A healthy Haven holiday

Incredibly, that wasn't the end of the holiday wins that year. In September, while we were actually on our Cornwall Cuddledry holiday, we heard that our eldest son, Joshua, had won a competition with Change4Life. It was a children's competition where you had to invent a game that would help you and your family stay healthy.

Joshua had come up with the idea of 'Frisbee Dodge' – a bit like dodgeball but using a Frisbee. We'd taken some photos of him playing it, added them to his write-up of the idea and sent it off.

The prize was a mid-week break at any Haven park, which had to be taken before the end of May the following year. Sadly, this ruled out being able to go when the outdoor pool was open in June, which Joshua was desperate to do, but we booked it for the following May, hopeful of good weather.

As it happened, May was cold and wet. Combined with the flare-up of back pain I was suffering due to my long-term arthritis, it wasn't the best of holidays. Nevertheless, it was still a break and very much enjoyed by the kids.

New York, New York (not)

The next year, I had one of my most exciting wins to date. This time, the promoter was Black Tower wine, and the prize came in two parts, the first of which was a trip for two to New York. As amazing as that sounds, and as much as I would have loved to go, the practicalities of finding childcare for three children, one of whom was still being breast-fed, made it all rather tricky.

Incredibly, however, and without us even asking, Black Tower very kindly offered us the cash equivalent so that we could put it towards a holiday of our own instead. We agreed that would be amazing. They worked it out to be £1,500. I was over the moon.

Not long after this, I saw that Pink Lining (one of my favourite changing bag brands) was doing an auction for CLIC Sargent, a wonderful charity that I also support. I watched as the auction proceeded throughout the day and felt frustrated that the bids that were going in were so low when it was for such a great cause.

After discussing things with my husband when he came in from work, we decided to donate some of the money that we had just won. As it was for such a great cause, we figured we could stretch to £150.

It was at this point that things got even more unbelievable. Whether you call it karma or simply the universe being on your side, what happened next was just amazing.

The money went into the auction. It was the highest bid for the bag, so we got it even though that was never the intention (indeed, as stunning as it was, I later gave the bag away).

Where the magic really happened was the phone call that came the very next day. The people at Black Tower rang out of the blue to say that they'd had a chat with their global head office and decided that £1,500 wasn't enough prize money and they were going to double it to a whopping £3,000! I was blown away. Not just because of the prize money, but because the increase was exactly ten times the amount we'd donated the evening before. It all seemed more than a coincidence to me – sowing and reaping. Sow kindness, reap kindness; sow generosity, reap generosity.

Despite my comping successes, my cash wins have always been few and far between, and as much as we would have loved to put the money aside towards bills and the mortgage, we felt it should go towards a holiday. As such, we put the money towards extending another prize later in the year so that we could take additional family members including Granny with us (see *The world's best restaurant* later in this chapter).

Never too old

As you've no doubt realised by now, there's no reason why lightning can't strike twice, and another massive holiday win was just around the corner.

This time, the promoter was McCarthy & Stone – a property builder specialising in retirement homes. They had been running a photo competition on their Facebook page entitled 'The Good Life' and they wanted to see photos of what 'the good life' meant to people.

I wanted my photo to feature someone in their target age range, and my husband's mother – with her fabulously white hair – immediately popped into my head. What with it being winter at the time, an idea about hair 'as white as snow' started brewing in my mind. We just had to wait … and hope … and pray for snow.

Luckily it came! We rushed around to Granny's house with the little one in tow and snapped a pic of Granny sledging in the garden with a nine-month old Trinity on her lap. It was actually not a pleasant day to be outdoors so the photos were really very rushed as I instructed Granny to whip off her woolly hat to show off her wonderful white hair.

Back home, the photos all looked ridiculously blurry. Feeling disappointed that my plan hadn't worked, I eventually settled for one that I figured would have to do.

On the one hand, it wasn't the best quality photo, but on the other this wasn't the sort of competition where entries would be judged based on their composition, quality and so on. I know nothing about exposure, ISOs and the like, so I make a point of avoiding such competitions. Photo competitions with this sort of theme, by contrast, usually mean the promoter is looking for a photo that captures something special. In this case, they wanted the essence of 'the good life', and ideally in a way that would appeal to their brand and what they stood for.

Along with the photo, I submitted the caption, 'Enjoying the good life with the grandchildren even when my hair is as white as the snow!'

I was particularly careful not to suggest that it was me in the photo. Rather, I wanted to suggest that for me, the good life would mean being able to do all manner of fun things whatever my age.

The deadline passed. Nothing was announced. On Facebook, the promoter responded to requests from people wanting to know who the winner was with something along the lines of 'we've contacted the winner directly'. I assumed it was someone else as I certainly hadn't heard anything.

Then one day, out of the blue, a white envelope appeared. I noticed the franking stamp on the corner saying McCarthy & Stone, but not for one moment did I think it was anything to do with the competition. After all, the deadline had passed and the winner had supposedly already been contacted. Surely this was just some promotional information because I'd entered the competition and failed to tick the box to opt out of receiving their marketing.

As I opened it, I couldn't believe my eyes.

It was a letter informing me that my photo had won! They put me in touch with Bath Travel (Now Hays Travel) where £3,000 worth of holiday awaited me.

Bath Travel were brilliant. Because we were unsure if we would be able to take the holiday before the official deadline date stated on the terms of the competition, they converted the prize into vouchers for us which had a much longer deadline of around four years into the future. Perfect! Lovely holiday prize money to use when we had the opportunity.

Summer at Sands
That June, I had another win. Trunki was running a competition on its blog in collaboration with Sands Resort in Cornwall. It was a simple 'leave a comment' competition where entrants had to explain what they thought their children would love most about Sands.

Whether it was random or judged I have no idea, but we got the winning e-mail (stuck in my spam filter – a perfect illustration of why it's important to check your spam folder regularly) saying we'd won a three-night break at Sands Resort.

As we were home-schooling, we took the opportunity to visit the very next month in July, and boy what a heatwave we had! It was hot hot hot! We had the most amazing time. We paid a little extra to upgrade to a larger family room. There was a separate sleeping area for the kids and a cot for Trinity. There was even a baby-listening service in the evenings. It was totally geared up for families, with so many activities onsite, an indoor and outdoor pool, and free wetsuit and surfboard hire when it was time to hit the beach.

That short break was one of our best holidays ever. We were blessed with the most incredible weather and Sands turned out to be all that we hoped it would be and more.

And yet, that wasn't our only holiday to Sands that year – we won another trip there a few months later (more on that in a bit!).

The world's best restaurant

Before starting this wonderful hobby, I would never have imagined having the opportunity to eat at the world's best restaurant. In fact, I'm not sure it would even have occurred to me to want to.

Comping, along with my other hobby of blogging, has really piqued my interest in food. As I spend more time online, I come across recipes that inspire me as well as competitions relating to food or recipe creation. I have loved learning more and more about food and cooking more than ever before.

A short while after I began to comp in earnest after my daughter was born, one website led to another – as it does on the internet – and I came across a blog called 'Superlucky' and a lady called Di Coke who was a complete expert in all things comping.

This was a massive eye-opener at the time. I was so excited to have found other people out there who enjoyed the same hobby as me.

It was on Di's Superlucky Facebook page that I saw her list a competition about a prize to Noma (the world's best restaurant at the time). It involved making a cookery video using frozen ingredients with Cool Cookery, an organisation that promotes the use of frozen food in the UK. Di mentioned that she'd won trips to Noma on two previous occasions so wasn't entering this one. Having a son who is a massive foodie who has dreamt of opening his own restaurant since he was a toddler, I knew that a visit to Noma would be a dream come true for him, so I had to enter on the off-chance that if I were to win, he would be my 'plus one'.

After a visit to the supermarket, during which I bought every single frozen ingredient I could think of, I proceeded to make 'herby hake with frozen vegetable cous-cous'. Looking back, my video isn't great – the sound quality is awful, I don't smile much and I sound boring. On top of that, the video is way too long – nearly 10 minutes. I've since learned short and snappy videos work far better for comps.

Fortunately – as commonly happens with video comps – there weren't too many entrants. In fact, I'm not sure there were even a dozen entries.

Possibly because of the variety of frozen ingredients that I'd used, I was shortlisted to the final four. But then came the curveball. Despite no mention of it in the T&C's, Cool Cookery decided to put the four finalists to the public vote.

I hate voting competitions. I always have and I always will. As regular compers know, they are flawed in any number of ways. Thankfully though, after a whole bunch of to-ing and fro-ing, the promoter decided to change it back to being judged.

Mine was the winning entry, but after the voting fiasco and having to have to complain to them, what was meant to have been a wonderful competition actually left me annoyed. Voting competitions are bad enough, but to introduce a voting element part-way through when it's not part of the T&C's, well … let's just say it's not cricket.

Noma is notoriously difficult to book a table at – especially tables for two – so we decided to pay extra so that my husband could join Daniel and me. After months of trying, the prize organisers eventually got us a reservation at the end of November.

One further complication was that I was still breastfeeding Trinity, so we used the Black Tower prize money I mentioned earlier in this chapter to pay for Trinity, Granny and our eldest son to come along to Copenhagen too. Although they didn't get to come to Noma, they still got to experience a little of Copenhagen with us. They actually enjoyed a meal at McDonald's that particular day instead – my eldest son's favourite!

Amazingly, there were two more holiday/short break wins in 2013 and a further three in 2014, but seven holidays in one chapter is quite enough for now.

CHAPTER 2

How did this happen?

So how did this story all start? Well, like many a tale, it was on a dark and stormy night. There was a knock at the door. At this time of night?! I thought to myself. Who could it possibly be?! And why are they saying my name?!

Actually, it can't have been that late – I was only about five or six – and it was only dark because it was winter. Nevertheless, I definitely heard my name.

Sure enough, a minute later, my mum came in holding one of those naff gift sets that you associate with grannies – you know the ones with two gold foil-wrapped bath cubes, hideously strongly scented and a circular rose soap – also overpoweringly smelly.

Well, I was delighted. My wish had come true. Earlier that day, we had stumbled across the local church fete and popped inside. I'd spotted this gift set on the raffle table and really wished hard for it. We'd gone home and thought nothing more of it and now here it was in my hands.

Good old mum used to allocate a raffle ticket to each of us whenever she bought them, writing our names on the back of each rather than just her name and this was my prize as *my* raffle ticket had been drawn!

Fast-forward some 30 years or so. Now I'm a mum of three. Life is hectic and busy.

When I was pregnant with my third baby, I was home-schooling the older two as my eldest has Asperger's Syndrome and school just wasn't working out for him.

We made the difficult decision to home-school and it turned out to be one of the best decisions we ever made. When it came to learning, we started out by making things as fun as possible. We tied in all our learning to topics that our children loved – namely computer games, and more computer games.

Maths was made up of counting that involved characters from their favourite games, stories were written about these characters, art would involve drawing or painting them. It proved to be the best way to break them into our emerging home-schooling routine.

When it was time to move on from that, I started to look online for resources – educational online games, worksheets, printables, story ideas, and so on. Every evening once the kids were in bed, I began looking online, preparing schoolwork for the following day. Spending so much time online meant that I was soon spotting competitions aimed at children.

We started combining our learning objectives with competition objectives, and started to see great results – both in the boys' learning and what they were winning.

For example, when learning about metaphors and similes, my son put them into a story about Hippo & Duck and won Silentnight's Book at Bedtime competition in 2012. The prize was an incredible stay at Alton Towers (which they kindly let us switch to the LEGOLAND Hotel for convenience), a new Silentnight bed and getting 150 copies of his story printed in book format! It was Jeremy Strong that had shortlisted the entries and, as a massive Jeremy Strong fan, my son was absolutely delighted.

We learned about poetry and creative writing. Both boys did really well in a Booktrust writing competition, winning tickets to the Wonderlands Book Festival at the British Library. The topic was 'My favourite place'. My eldest son came second place with a cheeky poem about the zoo, full of rhyming couplets. He won a small bundle of books for his efforts as well as the Wonderlands tickets. Meanwhile, my younger son wrote a poignant poem called 'The Sea', which related to the Granny he had never met who passed away before he was born. His poem was judged the winning poem in his age category and he won a massive pile of 52 books – one for every week of the year!

As both boys are avid readers, this was a dream come true. They even got to read their poems out in front of an audience in the storytelling tent at the festival. The Wonderlands Festival featured a number of renowned children's authors, and we even got to meet some of our absolute favourites, including Anthony Browne and Emily Gravett.

Another time, we learned about the environment, caring for our planet and the importance of buying products certified by the Forest Stewardship

Council. As there was also an adults' category in that competition, I got to enter too and I won Go Ape vouchers, lots of stationery and FSC goodies, proving it wasn't just the kids having all the luck.

You'll notice that the one thing all these competitions have in common is that they all involved a creative element of some sort, whether a story, a poem or artwork. And that is where our efforts have proved the most fruitful —where competitions require effort, the odds improve greatly, and 'luck' comes down to commitment, effort and talent.

By the time our daughter was born, I found myself in need of a creative outlet in order to escape from the daily grind of the newborn days, and that's when the hobby really shifted gear...

CHAPTER 3

A time for everything and a season for every activity

The seasons of life
Life is a series of seasons. Those seasons might relate to jobs, family life, education, voluntary commitments or something else, and it might not be obvious how long each one will last, but no matter what, none of them last forever.

The comping world is no different. There will be periods of great success, where the prizes roll in for weeks, months or even years. Likewise, there will be corresponding periods where the wins are few and far between, or may even dry up completely.

Sometimes all motivation and inspiration disappear for a while. Sometimes life's priorities, ill health or other crises take over and there is simply no time or energy left for comping. I've even reached a point where winning no longer made me happy.

The simple fact is that there is ebb and there is flow. As long as you can ride this seasonality and don't let the hobby become a ball and chain of obligation, but rather dip in and out of it as the seasons of your life allow, then it remains a fun and pleasure-filled hobby.

Baby, one more time
My comping season began when I was pregnant with my youngest child. As I've already mentioned, the sleepless nights and night-time feeding provided a great opportunity to scroll through Facebook and enter competitions – in particular, competitions for all kinds of baby essentials.

It was six years since the birth of our second son and we hadn't kept hold of our old baby items, so one of the things I really needed was a new buggy; likewise a stroller, for occasions where a bigger buggy would be impractical. As I'd never owned a decent changing bag, always relying on the freebie ones that get given to parents instead, I'd mentally added a decent changing bag to my wishlist too.

Spending so much time on Facebook, I had come across a number of companies selling stylish bangles and necklaces made from a rubbery kind of material that was safe for babies to chew. Knowing from experience how much babies love playing with objects not designed for them, such as car keys, mobile phones and jewellery, I really wanted to win some teething jewellery too.

There are of course plenty of other things that new babies need, from nappies to wipes to clothes and so on, but I had quite enough on my wishlist to get started.

Trinity was less than a month old when she grabbed her first prize. My favourite rabbit, Miffy, was celebrating her birthday, and the Miffy Facebook page was giving away a bumper amount of prizes.

At this point, I should confess that we are so obsessed with Miffy that we later became Official Miffy bloggers and we also made a visit to the Miffy Museum in Utrecht, the focus of one of our family holidays. That, however, is another story!

In this instance, we dressed Trinity in bunny ears (looking adorable!) and my husband took a great photo. I made that photo into a 'wanted' poster, surrounded by the words 'Wanted for impersonating Miffy' and uploaded it to the Miffy Facebook page. A few days later, Trinity had won a gorgeous Miffy sleepsuit and shoes, simply for looking cute.

Being such a Miffy fan, when I saw the competition to design a Miffy-themed birthday card, I thought it would be fun to design a few different cards. When choosing which one to enter into the competition, seasonality played a significant part of my strategy – it was 2012, the year of the Queen's Diamond Jubilee, and the whole country was decked out to the nines with union flags. With this in mind, I used one as the background to my 'Keep calm and Miffy on' design, and won a chocolate Miffy for my efforts.

A car-seat organiser came next, after I uploaded a picture of Trinity's first smile to Recaro's Facebook competition. The photo was taken when she was just a few days old, so it was almost certainly wind rather than a smile, but it did the job.

Facebook proved fruitful for a couple of cute items of clothing too: a little denim skirt and a stunning autumnal-coloured dress – brown with a gorgeous rose pattern on it – which I couldn't bear to part with when Trinity outgrew it so I made it into a skirt to last her a bit longer.

Then there was the food – not one, but two Organix hampers, one of which I won via the Tesco baby event giveaway and another via a parenting blog.

Next came the toiletries … so many toiletries!

In this regard, one of the most memorable wins was a year's supply of baby wipes. I've lost count of how many times Richard and I played the 'Colin the Crab' game on Asda's Facebook page. After days of getting the 'sorry you've not won – try again tomorrow' message, we found ourselves blinking in disbelief when the game finally came back with a 'winner' banner instead.

The prize was a year's supply of Johnson's baby wipes. Exactly how many wipes that would be, we were left to speculate. We figured that 52 packs – one for every week of the year – would have been a perfectly brilliant prize, and when the delivery man knocked on our door, he was indeed carrying one of the biggest boxes I've ever seen.

'So that's what a year's supply of baby wipes looks like!' I exclaimed. But it wasn't – there were another two boxes just like it waiting in the van!

When I explained that I'd won them, he was delighted to hear that people genuinely do win competitions, as he had never quite believed that the prizes were real and that promoters really were as good as their word.

'I've got triplets at home – I wish I'd won a year's supply of wipes!' he laughed.

As he unloaded the second enormous box, I told him to leave the third one in his van to take home for his triplets – he was thrilled.

So, did I actually manage to get any of my wishlist items?
- Big buggy – check! Not quite a competition prize, but a product trial of a Mutsy Evo buggy via Mumsnet. It was worth £399 and I got to keep it.
- Stroller – check! This came from a big giveaway that Kiddicare ran on Facebook. This had a royal jubilee design, which made it really special

as Trinity was born in 2012 – the same year as the Queen's Diamond Jubilee.

- Jewellery teethers – check! Thanks to persistently entering any and every competition for teething jewellery, I managed to win two competitions: one for a bangle and one for a necklace.

- Changing bag – check! This was an amazing Facebook competition with Munchkin in conjunction with Pink Lining (my favourite changing bag brand at the time). The promoter was running a week-long Facebook competition where entrants had to answer a daily question, and all the correct entries were put into a random draw at the end of the week. I made sure I answered the question each day to get the maximum number of entries that I was permitted, and I remember well the conversation I had with my husband when the winning e-mail came through…

Richard: (Sounding very bored) 'Oh, you've won a changing bag.'

Me: (Getting increasingly excited) 'A changing bag?! Which changing bag?!'

Richard: 'Just some changing bag … What does it matter which changing bag it is?'

Me: 'Of course it matters! Read the e-mail and tell me now please!'

Richard: 'It just says "a Pink Lining" changing bag.'

Me: (Squealing and jumping up and down) 'A Pink Lining changing bag!!! I've won a PINK LINING changing bag! OMG! OMG! OMG! I can't believe it!'

Richard: (Very puzzled that anyone can get this excited over a changing bag…)

Other baby-related prizes came in the form of a £50 JoJo Maman Bébé voucher from a blog giveaway, which I gave to a friend to spend on new maternity clothes that she needed, while both boys won cuddly JoJo bunnies by entering colouring competitions. Then, of course, there were the baby toiletries I won after uploading a seasonal Olympic-themed picture to Facebook and from leaving a comment on the Babipur blog. We also won a lovely raggy-tag blanket, a little Jubilee-themed comforter and a gorgeous pink blanket, which I ended up giving to a friend (but wish so much I'd kept for Trinity!).

Making the prizes even more lovely, people would stop me to comment on my changing bag, or compliment me on my teether jewellery, or tell me how great the buggy was. I'd be able to tell them that I won it all, along with the 'snoozeshade' cover for the buggy – a meshlike fabric cover to protect baby from the sun. That would certainly turn a few heads because although my baby could see out from the mesh, it was almost impossible to see into it, so people would often comment about that too – another excuse to tell them about my wonderful hobby!

Our season of schooling

The beauty of home-school is that everyone can choose their own way of doing it – from complete 'unschooling' to a replication of the school timetable and lessons at home. We had a down-the-middle approach where we'd set the kids certain 'educational' pieces of work to complete, including worksheets and working from textbooks, some topic-based or creative activities and free time, outings and adventures.

I would spend a lot of time online finding the types of work they 'should' be doing to make sure they didn't fall behind. The plan was that they would go back into the education system at some point, so it made sense to keep them up to speed with mainstream learning as well as the more flexible learning that we did. As I mentioned back in Chapter 2, while searching the internet for teaching resources, I would stumble upon all kinds of competitions for children, from writing poetry or stories to colouring, drawing, designing, and so on. It made complete sense to incorporate these competitions into the children's 'schoolwork' as it provided the added bonus of a potential prize for their efforts.

The boys enjoyed all manner of successes, including (but not limited to!) the following…

- Joshua was the overall winner of the very first 'Design a Squeeble' competition. The Squeebles apps are brilliant educational games where kids think they are gaming and having fun but actually do a whole lot of academic learning along the way. Joshua designed 'Raino', a yellow raindrop shaped Squeeble. His character was digitised and used in the subsequent Squeebles apps that have been developed. He also scooped himself a £15 Amazon voucher as part of the prize, but having his creation become part of history in the app was just the most epic feeling!
- When entering a colouring competition with Land of Sometimes, Joshua drew additional scenery to complement the rest of the colouring he did so it helped to make his entry stand out, and he won a beautiful framed illustration, a gorgeous art set and the Land of Sometimes story CD.
- In a design competition, Joshua designed a LEGO Chima vehicle, winning us a trip to Chessington. We had an awesome family day out,

being invited to the press room with journalists who were there to report on a new ride that had recently opened, followed by having the rest of the day to ourselves in the theme park and zoo.

- One of our favourite competitions, which ran over several years (and Joshua managed to get shortlisted to the finals a whopping three times) was a local 'Produced in Kent' competition where children were encouraged to use fresh seasonal fruit and veg to create 'artwork' on a certain theme. The very first year that it ran, Joshua was only four or five years old. He took some fruit and veg to create a clown's face with a big red tomato as the nose and got invited to the awards giving ceremony that year. In a future year, both Joshua and Daniel entered and again it was Joshua's Olympic-themed fencing entry that landed him a place in the finals. By this point, the competition had gained momentum and culminated in a 'live final' where the finalists had to recreate their artwork for a panel of judges. Joshua came second place. The year after that, he once again made it to the final. It was always a bit of an uncertain event in our family. Because of his Asperger's, we were very aware that at any point he could struggle with the pressure but amazingly once again he held it together, worked calmly creating his 'fruit and veg masterpiece' and this time landed first prize, with sculptor Guy Portelli being the lead judge that year. His prize included tickets to a local family attraction – the Museum of Kent Life – a signed Carl Warner print (food artist Carl Warner had been a judge in the previous years) and a bundle of gardening goodies.

- Another of my memorable moments from home-school was a cute little character that Daniel had drawn – a multi-coloured tortoise called Tank with a multitude of coloured squares covering his shell. I could immediately see his charm and knew he was onto a winner. He submitted him in a Tate Gallery competition which had the brief of designing a friend for 'Melvin the Monkey' of children's storybook fame. He won himself a signed copy of the book and a lovely family meal at the Tate.

And the actual seasons

Of course, the other element of 'seasonal' comping can relate to the actual seasons and times of year. Spring, Summer, Autumn and Winter all have their respective themes, from spring moments, to summer holidays, autumnal hygge, and in wintertime (as no promoter will let you forget) – Christmas. Throughout the year, there are countless opportunities to win seasonal giveaways both large and small. For example, a photo of Daniel rockpooling won a runner-up prize of a £10 COOK voucher.

On top of the actual seasons, there are also the special days, like Valentine's Day, Mother's Day, Bonfire Night, Pancake Day and so on.

Add in those other 'days', 'weeks' and even 'months' that have been introduced to raise awareness or simply for marketing purposes, such as 'Veganuary', Organic September, National Cupcake Week, Tea Day and so forth (the list really is endless!), and you have the makings of a whole calendar of comping opportunities to keep you busy.

It's a win-win situation as seasonal stuff gives companies great content for their marketing and social media, and at the same time gives compers and customers the opportunity to have fun and maybe even win prizes.

To give you an idea of just how much promoters love the seasons, let me share a few of our stories.

Father's Day
Father's Day, in particular, has proved particularly fruitful for us. For example, when we spotted a Father's Day drawing competition to win prizes at one of Heston Blumenthal's restaurants, The Hinds Head, we guessed that there would be plenty of entries for the kids' categories, but that the adult category might be less hotly contested. As I'm seriously rubbish at drawing, I pleaded with hubby to have a go, so he did a five-minute doodle of his dad walking the dog – and he won!

The promoter kindly swapped the prize (which for that category was a meal and cocktails) for a signed cookbook and a meal on a non-cocktail evening so that we could all go as a family. This, we did en-route home from our prize roadtrip with Laterooms.com (see Chapter 8 – When comping costs more).

Another fantastic Father's Day win came when I nominated Richard as deserving of a treat in Royal Mail's 'first-class dad' competition. I often find these competitions the hardest to enter because there are always people who do amazing things, whether that be helping others, coping with illness, overcoming adversity, or being generally fabulous all-rounders. What's more, these competitions tend to encourage sob-stories, and (like many compers) I really don't like that – there are so many people deserving of a treat out there – and most of them don't spend time moaning about their circumstances. So, I wanted to focus on the positives of what a brilliant dad my husband is and wrote about the voluntary work he had recently done with a children's charity which resulted in him helping to get nearly 100 children living in poverty sponsored.

The wording of the competition suggested there was an element of emotion to it, and for this reason I decided to share a story about something meaningful and caring that Richard had done in his own time; the fact it related to the 'fatherly' aspect of caring for kids helped make it relatable to Father's Day too. Taking the time to think strategically about this competition really paid off – Richard won an experience day, which he took in the form of an incredible helicopter ride.

Poetry Day

These days, special hashtagged days are ten a penny on social media, and yet it's not uncommon to find related competitions with relatively few entrants. For example, when Ecover promised a year's supply of washing-up liquid to the winner of its Poetry Day competition (and only a handful of people had bothered to enter) I knew this was a great chance to show off just what a big fan of Ecover I was already.

My entry went as follows:

> An ode to my fave cleaning brand,
> That uses nature's force,
> Plant extracts, and less chemicals It's ECOVER of course!
> My dishes get a fantastic treat,
> Getting washed so clean,
> And clean is my conscience too,
> With eco-credentials green.
> My laundry pile, squeals with delight,
> Knowing Ecover will wash clothes bright.
> And using Ecover's multi-surface spray, I hear the shower call out to say,
> 'Oi there sink, send it next my way!'
> Now my house feels palace grand,
> And with Mizu soap, I have princess hands.
> Even in the throne room, aka the loo,
> I hear the toilet bowl whisper, 'Ecover, thank you!'

Movember

Movember is always a great season. Alongside all the great work the charity does to raise awareness about men's health issues there are always lots of fun opportunities and competitions too.

One such promotion happened in 2013, when the official Movember cookbook, 'Cook like a Man', was published by Pan Macmillan. To celebrate the book's release, the publisher ran a competition offering four meals in top London restaurants.

The task required entrants to cook something from the cookbook and tweet either a photo or short video of said dish.

Even though the recipes were also available online, meaning that it wasn't strictly necessary to buy the cookbook, I figured that the competition still offered really good odds as (a) it still required no small amount of effort, (b) the prize was effectively restricted to people who could get to London easily and (c) not many people would bother trying to produce a video. With this in mind, we decided to have a go.

I came up with the idea of making the whole video Movember themed, and with a maximum of 12 seconds to tell the 'story', it had to be concise.

We bought the ingredients, cooked the meal and filmed a short clip of Richard in the kitchen preparing a romantic meal. The video then turns to me, sitting at a table set for two, and as I turn to face the camera, my hand-painted Movember moustache is revealed (see the video at https://tinyurl.com/winner-movember).

Not only did our video win, but it turned out that the prize was four times better than I was expecting! I'd understood that four winners would win a meal each, but actually the four meals were for a single winner – us!

National Insect Week
Yes, National Insect Week is indeed a 'thing' – who knew?! When I came across a competition to design a superbug, I knew it would translate really well into a home-school project to learn about insects and all their different features. This time, Joshua's superbug was the winner, bagging him a nice selection of insect-related books and stationery.

SPAM Appreciation Week
And if you thought National Insect Week sounded weird, how about SPAM Appreciation Week?!

This campaign has run for a few years now, but the first time we spotted it, we put all our efforts into a fantastically creative entry involving all the family. We made a video with us all dressed in SPAM colours as cheerleaders dancing and well, showing our appreciation of, SPAM.

Sadly, and despite our best efforts, we didn't win. The standard of entries was incredibly high, and the winning entry certainly was the most deserving – indeed, I remember the song and video well!

But all was not lost – the people at SPAM got in touch to say that they loved our entry so much, they'd decided to give us a runner-up prize of two tickets to a show at a theatre near us. When babysitting logistics proved too complicated, they kindly bought us cinema tickets for our family instead, which was great as it meant that we could all enjoy the prize.

CHAPTER 4

Christmas on the cheap

In the world of comping, some seasons are bigger than others. No season, however, is bigger than Christmas. For this reason, it qualifies for a chapter of its very own.

Now, I've never been a fan of Christmas – there's far too much over-commercialised fuss for my taste. I'm a real bah-humbug throughout November and December and frankly would gladly give the whole thing a miss.

However, because of this hobby of mine, I end up entering all sorts of weird and wonderful Christmas competitions. With a big smile on my face, I put all my effort into pretending I love Christmas. And you know what? Sometimes I genuinely end up enjoying myself after all!

Possibly the most fun our family had with Christmas comping actually came before my comping frenzy really started in earnest. It was during Moshi Monsters' heyday that we saw a competition to win a Nintendo 3DS. What with my kids being *the* biggest Moshi fans, I knew we had to give it a go. The challenge? To film yourself singing along to the Moshi Twistmas song.

I spent a whole weekend planning and making props and then a further weekend actually filming and editing video. The whole family got involved as we recreated the Moshi Twistmas video in as much of its entirety as we could manage. I was pregnant at the time and by the time we'd finished was absolutely exhausted.

The video was featured on the Moshi Monsters blog page, and with over 90 million people using Moshi Monsters at the time, the YouTube hits grew exponentially for the first few days, hitting 8,000 views, then 16,000 then just over 30,000 ... 60,000, until we reached over a whopping 100,000 hits, before gradually settling down.

A bit like Christmas, though, there was an anti-climax ... we didn't actually win. But it really was enormous fun taking part.

The great thing about being a comper at Christmas is that there is a massive flurry of competitions around that time. In addition, people are often busy with Christmas parties, so even the non-Christmas related competitions that happen to have a December deadline may end up with far fewer people entering than they would at other times of the year.

Our first proper comping Christmas was Trinity's first Christmas in 2012. One of the first prizes we won was not actually destined for me or the kids but was a £100 Co-op voucher and party pack comprising Christmas crackers, table cloths, and paper plates and cups where entrants had to nominate a good cause. At the time, we were part of a home-school group specifically for children with autistic spectrum disorder (ASD) and I knew that they liked to have a Christmas celebration each year, so we nominated them. I won the voucher, bought lots of party food from the Co-op with it, and the kids who were part of the ASD home-school group had a fabulous time.

That Christmas, I was spending so much time on Facebook that I also scooped a few little prizes …

- A £20 photo voucher by uploading a Christmas photo (I had one of Trinity in a Christmas hat that I'd taken back in October in preparation!).
- Cinema tickets.
- A box of foliage and 'natural decorations' from Rocket Gardens – although this arrived too close to Christmas to be put to good use in our house. Even the local churches had done their flower arranging by then, but I was able to pass the prize to a friend who was doing a floristry course.
- A changing mat and cloth nappy from a snowflake-making competition, which I won by cutting out the promoter's name (FuzziBunz) and hanging it on the Christmas tree along with other snowflakes.
- Baby shampoo and wash mitt from a competition where entrants had to post a photo of their Christmas tree.
- £50 to spend at Cuddledry – I dressed Trinity with homemade reindeer horns and painted on a little red nose and uploaded a photo to Facebook (they must have had a soft spot for beautiful Trinity, especially after winning our cottage holiday with them earlier that year!).
- Laura Lee Designs had a colouring competition that adults could enter too – I won an apron, while the kids each got a £5 voucher to spend as runners-up.

- Pushchair Trader had a random draw where I won a £25 voucher to spend at Bamboo Baby – I picked a lovely pink cardigan for Trinity (unfortunately, however, I had to pay the postage on that prize, taking a little of the gloss off the win).
- Joshua also won another colouring competition. In this instance, the promoter hadn't stated what the prize would be, so he was a bit disappointed to receive a chalkboard and chalks from the 99p Store; still, he enjoyed the glory of the win! The boys had a more positive experience with British Gas, however, winning a decent board game each – Operation and Kerplunk – for their colouring efforts.

Away from Facebook, the bigger prizes came from competitions that required a little more effort. For example, Debenhams wanted to see photos of Christmas indulgence – the theme and prizes changed slightly each week throughout December.

Of course, the great thing about competitions that run for several weeks is that it gives the opportunity to see the winning entries, learn from them, and to submit an entry that is more likely to appeal to the promoter.

I uploaded a photo of me in the bath with a Santa hat, holding a mince pie and a glass of mulled wine (and plenty of bubbles of course to cover up!), along with the caption of 'Mulled wine, mince pies and a spot of pre-Christmas pampering'. As that week's prize was a £300 bundle of beauty goodies, the photo and caption were a good fit with the theme and the prize.

I've tried using a similar photo in other comps since but with no luck. I guess there was just a certain time and place for a photo of me in the bath and that was it!

Three of our biggies that Christmas came from writing blog posts. I have had a lot of success in competitions aimed at bloggers, so even if it is just a hobby blog about whatever you are interested in, blogging definitely opens up new opportunities in the comping world.

It is always worth making the effort with creative and effort-based competitions at Christmas time because so many people are so busy making Christmas plans and doing their Christmas shopping that they simply can't find the time to enter.

This is another time when comping through the year can be really helpful. I asked the kids if they preferred to receive little prizes throughout the year or to get lots in one go at Christmas. They unanimously agreed that a bumper Christmas was far more exciting. With this in mind, I squirrel away prizes throughout the year and, when the season finally comes, end up hardly spending a thing.

Christmas – for free!

In 2013, Christmas arrived all wrapped up and ready for us. As I had become accustomed to doing, I'd saved a few books that I'd won earlier in the year and hidden them away for Christmas.

Daniel, meanwhile, had won a design-a-wigwam competition. Knowing most kids would draw a design on paper and a few might even make a model from cardboard, I encouraged Daniel to think of something really unique. One of his passions is food and cookery so he decided to make his wigwam from chocolate. A visit to the shop to buy some chocolate Matchmakers, some marshmallows and some Christmassy sprinkles and he was ready to go. We snapped a few photos of his fab little wigwam and sent off the best pic.

The prize was an awesome children's wigwam, which I stashed away when it arrived in order to do the big reveal at Christmas. Once he opened it, I told him he had won it and he was thrilled.

That year, Daniel also won tickets to see Michael Rosen's incredible *Centrally Heated Knickers* show at the Science Museum. Daniel had written a short poem called 'Robot Dragons' for the competition and had done it in a matter of minutes. In addition to tickets, his poem won him a signed copy of *Centrally Heated Knickers* and a meet-and-greet with Michael Rosen himself!

Unfortunately, no-one at the Science Museum knew anything about the book. However, as it happened, the lovely Michael Rosen came out after the show to chat and do book signings for anyone who had brought their own books with them, so we did get to meet him after all!

Back home, I dropped a quick e-mail to the contact who had informed us of the prize win, just to let them know that the books weren't available. I think the prize had been organised by the publisher in conjunction with the Science Museum, so the arrangements had somehow fallen through the gaps.

They were incredibly apologetic and sent Daniel an awesome parcel and covering letter addressed to him by way of apology. Inside the parcel was an extremely thoughtful gift … a remote-controlled robot dragon! Given that Daniel's original poem had been about robot dragons, this was just amazing. They also included a signed copy of *Centrally Heated Knickers* for both Daniel and Joshua. That really is some apology! This, of course, got all hidden away until Christmas, making for a wonderful surprise.

And last, but certainly not least, we had entered a blogging competition with an online toy company (sadly no longer in existence), where the post had to list not just what the children wanted, but why. Not only did we win everything on the list, but everything was gift-wrapped too! It made for the biggest pile of presents under the tree that we've ever had. It was totally amazing and extremely tricky to keep quiet until the big day.

In short, our children had a truly magical Christmas in 2013, and it hadn't cost us a penny!

Oops, I did it again!

By the time we got to Christmas 2014, the kids had certainly got used to getting amazing presents at Christmas. They had also learned that when mum found them a competition to enter, it was worth putting in the effort. Halfords was running a weekly competition in the run-up to Christmas with different prizes each week. This was a competition for children and required writing a letter to Santa.

Joshua wrote a great letter, joking about how he wanted to 'sack' mum and dad for never bringing him the presents he wanted – and then drawing a Santa sack with mum and dad in it. He entered during the first week, before many people had heard about the competition, and won himself a fab skateboard worth around £70!

I mention this here under the 'Oops I did it again!' heading because the following year, Trinity used the same strategy of getting her entry in early. Again, it was the first week, so before many other people had seen the competition, and she won herself a brand new bike!

So, it is possible for lightning to strike twice, as they say – two wins with the same company in two consecutive Christmases. In fact, the wigwam that we won in 2013 was also Daniel's second win from the same company – Big Game Hunters. The previous year, they'd had a competition to design a dream house where the prize was a beautiful outdoor playhouse. He'd thrown together a last-minute entry – not even bothering to colour it, but instead scanned it into the computer and added a splash of colour digitally. I think his laziness worked in his favour by making his entry stand out because he'd used both drawing skills and computer skills. It also helped that he had drawn a Christmas scene in his dream house, saying he'd like it to be Christmas all year round. That element of seasonality must've got everyone in the Christmas mood and got his entry picked as the winner.

CHAPTER 5

A family affair

As you will no doubt have realised by now, my comping hobby has very much become a family thing. My husband and kids all know that when mum gets a bee in her bonnet about entering a particular competition that needs their involvement, they'd better get on board!

Most the time it's fun for everyone involved, but organising that many people for a family-themed competition is not without its headaches. When that happens, I remember the words of a good friend: 'when the fun stops, it's time to stop' – and we all take a break!

Broadly speaking, family competitions fall into four main categories:
- comps that require a team effort;
- family comps where the kids are centre stage;
- comps for kids only; and
- comps for all ages.

Team effort competitions
Some competitions require the whole family to be involved. Most commonly, the entry mechanic takes the form of a family photo or a video, such as the SPAM video mentioned in Chapter 3.

Putting the kids centre stage
It is always worth making the child the focus of the photo or video if it resonates well with the promoter's brand, their campaign message or even the prize itself. We do this a lot on our parenting blog when there are blogger competitions as these tend to be themed around parenting topics or food products that appeal to kids. One that springs to mind is the Petit Filous 'Mix up the Magic' campaign, where our blog post that included videos of the kids taking centre stage scooped the top prize of a £500 shopping voucher.

Competitions for children

Some creative competitions come with age limits or age categories and are aimed squarely at children. Common examples include drawing, colouring or writing stories or poetry. When we were home-schooling, these kinds of competitions formed a big part of our curriculum; for example, we would learn some aspect of writing or poetry and the kids would put it into practice via a competition entry, or we'd try out some new art materials or painting techniques and they'd use those new skills to enter a competition.

I also try to keep track of which photos the kids have taken because sometimes there will be photo competitions where the kids need to be *behind* the camera taking photos – perhaps of wildlife or a family holiday.

Other times, kids need to be the subject of the competition, for example, a baby photo contest such as the Cuddledry one that we won, or a true story about something that has happened involving them, such as a funny thing they have said or done.

Comps for all ages

One of my most favourite types of competition is where the age categories encompass both children's age groups and adults too. We love these occasions as our family get to have quality time together as we all sit around the table, each working on our own colouring (such as with the Laura Lee Designs competition I mentioned in the last chapter) or poetry (like Divine's annual poetry competition) or some of the short-story competitions that are open to all age groups.

I have especially fond memories of Innocent Smoothies running such a competition a few years ago. The brief was to design the different letters for their iconic fridge magnets. It was a very kid-friendly comp, so I got in touch with them to double check they were happy for adults to enter too. After they confirmed that this was indeed fine, the four of us all sat around the table having great fun designing the magnets (Trinity was just a young baby then so obviously couldn't take part). A few weeks after the closing date, each of us received an individually addressed letter containing £16 of Innocent vouchers, making a whopping total of £64 of vouchers! It was a fab prize, made all the more special by us all taking part, and all winning a prize.

CHAPTER 6

Comping smarter not harder

Luck is a numbers game. There's no great secret: the more competitions you enter, the more you are likely to win. It really is as simple as that.

'Well, duh, that's obvious', you sigh. But it bears repeating because one of the most common conversations that I have had with people when they hear about this hobby of mine goes something like this ...

Me:	(describing one of my wins – perhaps a holiday, perhaps a kitchen mixer, perhaps something smaller that I get equally excited about).
Friend:	You are SO lucky. I NEVER win ANYTHING! It's so unfair.
Me:	So, when did you last enter a competition?
Friend:	Actually, I don't really enter competitions.
OR	
Friend:	Well, I did enter a raffle once a few years ago but I didn't win anything.
OR	
Friend:	Well, I do enter the lottery but I've never won that.
Me:	(*exasperated sigh!*) But how do you expect to win if you barely or never enter/play the lottery when the chances of winning are so small? (*delete as appropriate*)

The odds of winning lotteries are of course famously poor, which is one of the reasons I don't buy lottery tickets. In fact, I rarely pay to enter any kind of competition, unless it's in aid of a charity or good cause that I support. As a rule, though, I stick to competitions that are free to enter – and there are plenty of them out there!

Some compers enter hundreds of competitions each and every day. This is certainly one way to scoop prizes, but the reality is that it's very time-consuming. It's also mind-numbing – sitting at the computer filling in your name and address a hundred times a night isn't for everyone.

This is where the use of strategy comes in.

As any seasoned comper will tell you, the harder it is to enter a competition, the better the odds will be!

Indeed, for me, the biggest satisfaction I get from this hobby is not the actual winning of prizes, it's the *creative* element that some competitions demand: to really get under the skin of a brand and understand what they're about, their values, their target customers, their current campaigns … and then craft a (hopefully) winning entry that will stand out among other entries *because* it embodies what that brand is all about.

When I win those types of competition – when I've nailed what that brand is looking for – that's when I feel I've really earned it and deserve it. That's what gives me the greatest satisfaction.

As a comping nerd, another thing that brings me satisfaction is knowing when I've managed to comp in the most time-efficient way possible. This is particularly important during quiet patches when it's tempting to spend more time comping in order to secure that elusive win.

The truth is, there are better ways to use that time. For example, it's important to plan ahead. This is something I'm rubbish at. I tend to think of one comp at a time – use all my creative juices on one project before turning my thoughts to the next. That's not always smart. A much better idea is to look ahead in the diary to identify any forthcoming comping deadlines and whether there are any opportunities to double-up to maximise your efficiency.

For example, in summer 2013, Sands Resort Hotel (where we'd already enjoyed an amazing break that year thanks to Trunki – see Chapter 1) ran a Facebook competition where entrants had to upload a photo of their 'beach art'. The example they showed was of a fantastic mermaid made of stones and seaweed and driftwood. Immediately, a load of sandcastle photos were posted by people who already had photos that they could recycle.

I was keen to attempt some proper 'beach art' for my entry, but time was ticking on and we don't live near a beach.

In the meantime, I had identified another Facebook competition, this time with Green People Organic. Back then, the company had a separate Facebook page for its 'Organic Babies' brand and had launched a competition to showcase its products being used 'out and about' that summer.

The obvious choice was their sun cream. Annoyingly, I'd just finished our last tube of that brand of sun cream and as I only put an order in with them once in a while, there was no time to get more before the deadline. I had to put my thinking cap on and see which of their other products we used that could go 'out and about' with us. I then remembered that they have a lovely soothing baby salve that I use to stop my daughter getting dry skin, so that was the product to take with us.

On our final chance before summer was out, we headed to the beach over the August bank holiday weekend. I got my pic of Trinity holding the Organic Babies baby salve – she's always been so adorably photogenic, and I was happy with the photo we got.

Then onto sand art. On a sandy beach with not many pebbles, this was a bit of a challenge! However, inspired by the shape of a rock that looked like it could be a seahorse's head we started work on shaping some seaweed and making it look like a seahorse.

Having taken a couple of photos of it, it was still lacking something. There was no 'wow' factor – so to show that we'd made this seahorse beach art specifically for the Sands competition, we wrote 'Sands' in the sand above the seahorse. Then I was happy. Two good entries for two different comps and all on the same day while having a lovely day out at the beach.

And the icing on the cake was … we won both!

I'm lucky enough to have won lots of creative competitions like this, but three in particular come to mind.

My favourite creative wins
Black Tower – when a weakness can be a strength
Back in 2013, Black Tower ran a competition to design a special edition bottle for their wine. I'd long been a fan of the iconic black and white bottle of this fabulous fruity wine so the idea really appealed to me.

My daughter was just a baby at the time, under a year old, and I was still home-schooling my boys. I knew I would need some thinking time to come up with a good idea and yet the days were flying by as the competition deadline loomed.

The obvious themes with the black and white bottle were things that were black and white – zebras, penguins, newspapers, and the like. But they were all rather random ideas and none of them captured the essence of the brand.

The deadline drew near (I think it was the day before the deadline – talk about cutting it fine!) and as Trinity had her afternoon nap that day I knew I'd reached the point of 'now or never'. I got onto the Black Tower website and totally immersed myself in it, asking myself a serious of questions:

- What is this product all about?
- What does the branding look like?
- Who is the product aimed at?
- What is their strapline/tagline?
- What is the 'tone of voice'?

In the end, it was the 'Easy ends the day' tagline that caught my attention.

Whilst the brand was an iconic established brand that became popular in the seventies, more recently it seemed to be targeting younger consumers. In my mind, I visualised a young working professional, could be male or female – Black Tower seemed to hold equal appeal to both – arriving home after a long day at work. Perhaps they worked in the city. Perhaps they had to stay late at work to meet a deadline. Getting home represents a time to unwind. And what better way to unwind than by listening to music.

Perhaps instead of heading home, they're meeting with friends or colleagues, enjoying a sophisticated evening out in a bar with live piano music playing in the background.

And that was it. With the distinctive black and white bottle still in my mind, the idea of black and white piano keys wrapping around the bottle was born.

As I sketched out my design, not only did I discover how hard it is trying to draw the outline of a bottle, but I also began to have doubts.

As much as my idea felt the 'right' idea to go with, seeing my piano keys drawn onto the bottle outline on the piece of paper in front of me somehow didn't seem enough. It just didn't shout 'wow' or make the bottle truly special. The piano keys on the black part of the bottle looked good but the rest just looked too plain. My brain started whirring around the theme of music and relaxing at the end of the day. I've always thought musical scales look beautiful (even though I don't actually have a musical bone in my body), but rather than a straightforward ordinary musical scale, I decided upon the idea of a musical scale unravelling around the bottom (white/clear) part of the bottle to denote the relaxing theme.

Rather than 'proper' notes and musical symbols I used poetic licence to draw my own unique selection of notes including a few stars and random unravelling twists and curls.

With my design complete, I scribbled a few notes around the edges of the paper to explain my reasoning for the various parts of the design, scanned the whole thing in and uploaded it on the competition page.

I was not tech-savvy enough to use the Black Tower design app, hence the hand-drawn design. And I also must point out that while people may think of me as 'creative', when it comes to actual drawing and art, my skills really suck. But I did my best and figured that in the unlikely event of being selected, Black Tower would have access to a team of techie design people who could easily replicate the design into the digitised format they required. First came the news that I'd been shortlisted. I was in shock. The company wanted a bit of background info about me and to check it was all my own design and not copied from anywhere.

It meant so much to me to be shortlisted. I think I even told them that I didn't care about winning as it felt so amazing to have been shortlisted as I was thrilled that they liked my design.

Next came the news that my bottle had been chosen as the overall winning design.

For anyone out there who doubts their own abilities – this next sentence is for you to bear in mind … Sometimes something that we see as a weakness can actually give us an advantage, an edge or point of difference to make us stand out. The design that I had hand-drawn because I lacked the skills or ability to do it digitally, is one of the things the promoter loved about it.

They felt it made the design truly unique and that it would stand out on the supermarket shelves because of it.

Soon I found myself holding one of the half-a-million bottles of Black Tower wine that had been produced with *my* design on it. *My* design. My exact design – not digitised to recreate my ideas – but an actual facsimile of my hand-drawn work.

For the next few months, I'd head to the wine aisle in any supermarket I visited, taking selfies and staring in amazement that *my* bottles of wine were on the shelves. Even though as a home-schooling housewife with a young family, I personally didn't fall into the target market I had imagined when creating the design; even though I didn't have the technical skills to create a digital design so had drawn by hand; even though I'd scribbled down my notes in rushed handwriting before my baby awoke from her nap (which they had then used that same handwriting of mine on the actual bottles too!); against all these odds, my bottle design had won. What's more, as I mentioned in Chapter 1, this wasn't the only element of this remarkable prize.

Even writing this several years later it seems like something impossible had happened to me.

That is the beauty of this hobby. Sometimes the impossible *can* happen.

Patak's Curry King – getting the target market right
Where a competition winner is randomly drawn, then the company doesn't get to choose whether the winner is male or female, young or old, rich or poor, what type of work they do and so on.

Where a competition is judged, however, there is always the potential for the promoter to be influenced by the entrant's demographic when choosing a winner. Whether this is a conscious or subconscious decision on their part matters not – the potential remains.

Most brands have a reasonably good idea of who their main customers are. They'll often have sophisticated ways of targeting their customers and potential customers. As well as by general demographic factors, they may go further and categorise by behaviours, attitudes, hobbies and so on.

My experience suggests that, by reading between the lines of a competition, it is possible to get a feel for who that target audience is.

We love curry, so when we spotted that Patak's was looking for a curry lover to become its chief curry taster for a year, input into their new product development ideas and win a meal cooked for them by Anjali Pathak, we knew we had to enter.

Reading between the lines of the competition brief, there was one sentence that described the prize to include a meal cooked for you and your 'mates'.

Somehow, the language used conjured up the image of a group of lads enjoying a curry and a beer.

So, despite my own love of food and curry, we made the strategic decision that my husband would enter as we felt he would be likely to fare better. There was no guarantee, of course, but based on the way the competition had been described, we figured it was worth a try. So, together we wrote a (cheesy) laddish poem about the various reasons Richard adored curry.

A delighted Richard had made the shortlist – they had loved the curry poem!

A series of radio interviews, press articles and further interviews with Patak's brand agency ensued and Richard was selected as the overall winner and dubbed the King of Curry.

His prize included a year's supply of Patak's ingredients, a New Product Development (NPD) tasting session, a masterclass and dinner cooked at our home with Anjali Pathak for a group of our friends, and a further spice masterclass with Patak's NPD chef Manish.

This prize provided a wonderful whirlwind of experiences, and Richard was the envy of all his friends! After seeing the story in our local paper, he would even get stopped in the street and congratulated on his new job. People actually thought it was a new job to replace his day job. Sadly not, but it was a wonderful experience for him and for our family.

The Baaftas – playing the odds
I only recently learned to cook. After leaving home to go to university, I survived on pasta, toast and Findus Crispy Pancakes. I suspect I was not the only student to do so. It was only after having my own family that I started to realise that bringing up kids on ready meals and takeaways was not the wisest thing to do. So, I began to cook. Just the standard stuff to start with – spag bol, pasta bake, frozen fish fingers and peas. Gradually, however, my repertoire increased, and even more recently I found that the more time I spent online comping and blogging, the more inspiring recipes I would find and want to try out.

Given how much I used to dread cooking and baking, this progress is nothing short of incredible. Even more miraculous, however, is the fact that I've managed to win a number of cookery competitions too!

One such win was when Welsh Lamb was running a 'Baafta' awards cooking competition, where participants had to submit photos of lamb dishes they had created. There were a whopping 40 prizes on offer – ten for each of the four categories. Each prize consisted of £100 worth of Welsh lamb, a cookery book and a trophy too.

I soon got cooking to create some dishes inspired by Welsh Lamb. I came up with three that I entered into three of the categories, while Richard entered one of his dishes, a lamb curry, into the fourth category – the Mid-week Masterpiece category. In this way, between us we had entries in each of the categories. The competition was not limited to one entry per person, so we made the most of opportunity. We also entered each of our recipes into a different category to increase the odds of winning. With 40 prizes on offer, I really hoped that one of us would win.

We each received an e-mail telling us we had won: me in the Welsh Wizardry category with my lamb and feta pastry wheels and Richard in the Mid-week Masterpiece category with his lamb curry. So, between us we'd scooped two of the prizes – a whopping £200 worth of lamb and a trophy each. We cleared out the freezer to make space and it was great to have so much wonderful quality meat to keep us going for quite some time.

Time to swerve
Another aspect of comping smarter is recognising that the supply of competitions is inexhaustible – it's simply impossible to enter them all! With this in mind, I find it helpful to have no-go areas. No-go areas are based on very personal decisions, so what's right for one person will never be right for everybody. The key thing is that by setting such boundaries, you've got more time to focus on the competitions that really interest you.
These days, there are five areas where I avoid comping. Before I talk about these in more detail, however, I should reiterate that I do this for personal reasons, and that I would never judge anyone for doing differently!

Halloween
As a family, we don't feel it's right to celebrate Halloween on account of its roots. Despite many claiming it is 'harmless fun', we know of examples where Halloween activities have caused years of pain following the Halloween-related death of a loved one.

In the year that I first *really* got into comping and was spending hours on Facebook, Halloween became impossible to avoid, and despite my strong feelings about it, the temptation of entering a creative competition was too much. I created a couple of what I saw as 'harmless' entries based on my baby daughter looking cute with pumpkins rather than anything gross or gory. And I won two of those competitions that year.

This left me wrestling with my conscience because I knew that by entering those competitions I was supporting the concept of celebrating Halloween. For this reason, every October since then I reduce my time on Facebook and avoid Halloween competitions simply because that's what fits with my own personal beliefs.

Gambling

Some may argue that comping by its very nature is a form of gambling – only with your time rather than your money, spending many hours on a hobby that may not result in any 'reward'.

Personally, I don't see my hobby in that way. For me, the gains often come from the creative process involved in effort-based competitions. For other competitions, I make sure I enjoy the interaction with various brands on social media. Even with the 'form-filling' comps, I have come across brands and products that I may never have otherwise heard of and that to me holds value in itself.

I've made the decision to steer clear of competitions that involve paying to enter, whether that be texting a premium number or buying a National Lottery ticket. That said, I do make an exception for charities and good causes close to my heart, where my primary motivation is to donate to the charity.

Although I don't enter many of them, I will also buy the odd product for a 'purchase necessary' competition, but only if it is something I will use anyway, even if it is a different brand to my normal one.

I will also occasionally purchase food items or 'props' with a particular competition in mind. This means there can sometimes be a financial 'cost' to this hobby, but again, as long as these things don't go to waste (e.g. the food will be eaten regardless) then I'm happy to do this.

Voting with my feet

There are occasions when the promoter or the prize leaves me with conflicted feelings.

At the time of writing, the global political climate is undergoing a period of uncertainty. So, when Heart Radio ran its 'Faces for Florida' promotion again, we initially put in a couple of entries. However, as the political climate became less and less stable, we decided that we no longer had any desire to visit the States at the current time, so didn't bother with any further entries.

I avoid also competitions with a voting element. I have seen far too much upset and negativity caused by these types of competition so I walk away. Most of the comping community I interact with can't stand voting competitions, so I remain hopeful that if enough people stop entering them, then the promoters will have to stop running them.

Too many wins with one company
Thanks to the law of probability, or possibly pure talent and skill (ahem!), it is possible to end up having a flurry of wins with one particular brand.

This happened a few years ago when I happened to win a lot with Trunki. I love their products anyway and am a loyal customer of theirs, but the wins went like this:

- Holiday to Sands after leaving a blog post comment (not sure if it was random or judged but my comment was picked as the winning one).
- Trunki Paddlepak won via Rafflecopter on a blogger's competition but with the prize fulfilled by Trunki.
- Trunki ride-on storage crates and Crayola goodies won via random draw on the Trunki blog.
- Trunki Gruffalo wash-bag won via another blogger's competition – judged by the blogger not by Trunki.
- Trunki ride-on case in customised colour scheme after my son drew his own Trunki design for their Facebook competition.

At that point, I knew it was time to take a break from the wonderful Trunki giveaways. Even though the vast majority of these were randomly picked, I found myself feeling bad for winning so much with them. I must emphasise though that the experience has made me a mega-loyal customer of theirs, and when they launched their Jurni range I was first in the queue to buy one!

Is it worth it?
Occasionally, there may be another reason *not* to enter a competition. Back in 2014, Nectar ran its annual competition to find Britain's savviest family. We were delighted to have made the shortlist of finalists, along with seven other families.

With a prize package worth over £10,000, we had to give it our best shot. All finalists had to commit to a period of writing blog posts under different headings (e.g. leisure, shopping, etc). In return, everyone received a small amount of Nectar points and a camera to take photos and record videos for those posts.

Sadly, the camera was a piece of junk – the photo quality was so blurry and poor that we used our own camera for all the images and video we needed. Each family put in a lot of effort. Of course, we all knew there could only be one winner, but having got through to the final, we kept on, doing our best, pulling out all the stops in the hope that maybe just maybe…

In the end, another family's excellent efforts won the contest, although it's fair to say that the standard of effort was so high that any of the families could have been worthwhile winners. But knowing what I now know about the amount of effort involved in taking part, would I do it again? … No!

In fact, I wasn't the only one to feel this way. One of the other finalists got in touch with me to say how they felt like it had all been a waste of time because of all the effort involved with no 'runner-up' prizes for the other finalists, who had put in just as much effort as the winning family.

Had the promoter just put a little more thought into it, perhaps ensuring that the finalists all received a decent camera or another worthwhile prize just for taking part, in order to reflect the level of time and commitment involved, then perhaps they would have been left with eight happy families rather than one happy family and seven not-so-happy families.

I put it down to experience and I'm now much more wary about knowing exactly what I am committing to if I find myself as a finalist again.

CHAPTER 7

Experiences vs products

I'm often asked whether I prefer winning products or experiences. There are certainly loads of factors to consider here, but over the years I've found that experiences can sometimes be the most exciting prizes of all. This is certainly the case with 'money can't buy' prizes, such as meeting a celebrity or getting the VIP treatment at a fancy event.

That said, even 'experience day' prizes that money *can* buy feel like a real treat when they are something that you would not ordinarily treat yourself to. We've enjoyed some overnight stays and shows that we would not typically have attended but have made the extra effort to book babysitters to ensure we really got to enjoy the prize.

There are also those unusual activities that would never even occur to me to try – like making sushi, decorating cupcakes, taking a ride in a helicopter or getting up close with some birds of prey – so it's great to get out of my comfort zone and try new things.

The other thing with experience prizes is that they come with a triple whammy of enjoyment. To start with, there's the joy and buzz of discovering you have won. Next, there's the build-up of anticipation when you book the experience and make arrangements. And finally, there's the day itself, which in some instances can be so fantastic as to be thoroughly surreal – certainly, we've had a couple of experiences that felt like dreams come true!

Moshi Monsters Music Rox launch party
Back in the heyday of Moshi Monsters, my two sons were the biggest Moshi Monsters fans. As such, when I saw a competition to win VIP tickets to the Moshi Music Rox launch party, I had no real choice but to enter.

We had to come up with the three questions that we most wanted to ask Mr Moshi. Our boys had been lucky enough to meet Mr Moshi before as Joshua had been invited to Moshi HQ while home-schooling. He'd designed hundreds of new Moshling characters just for fun because he enjoyed doing so and when we sent them into Moshi HQ they kindly invited him to visit Moshi HQ and meet the team there. That day was amazing. But that was another story and wasn't the prize win.

We came up with the questions and e-mailed them in. Then, when we received news that our three questions had won we all screamed with delight and genuinely leaped up and down.

The person who was judging the entries was new to Moshi HQ and so had no idea about just what massive fans we were.

I was heavily pregnant with Trinity when the party date rolled around and I made my own bespoke Moshi-themed t-shirt to wear.

We had the most amazing evening and Mr Moshi recognised us when we got to meet him, which was super cool and in all the excitement we forgot to ask him the questions! We also bumped into Sophie Ellis-Bextor (who was as heavily pregnant as I was but looked a million times more glamorous) and McFly were there too.

Thankfully, there was a piece featured in the following months Moshi magazine and Mr Moshi did get to answer the questions there. They used our photos and the piece we'd written about the party in the magazine too. The kids were delighted!

Meeting the queen of baking – Mary Berry

Along with going to school with Katie Price and stalking Boyzone round a Brighton nightclub in my teens, meeting Mary Berry has to be one of my top 'claim to fame' moments. It wasn't even my own prize win but my son's win – who was eight years old at the time.

He'd entered the BBC Good Food Bakes and Cakes Show baking competition. There were competitions for both adults and juniors, with each of those categories divided into 'bakes' and 'cakes'. As my own baking leaves a lot to be desired, I didn't even enter – all our hopes were pinned on Daniel.

To enter the competition, he baked some chocolate cookies and sent off the photos. Then we heard he had been shortlisted. He would need to bake them again and bring them to the Bakes and Cakes Show to be tasted and judged on the Saturday of the show.

With school's permission, he took the Friday afternoon off school to do his baking. I remember that afternoon distinctly as our back fence was being replaced and I was torn between being on hand for Daniel while he was cooking and responding to the builders' questions and queries and making them cups of tea.

As it happened, Daniel didn't need any help. He's been really confident in the kitchen since he was tiny so he just got on with making his cookies.

The next morning was an early start – the cookies needed to be at the show before 9am. Trinity, who was only two at the time, woke up looking very poorly. I was feeling pretty tired having woken up so early and for a few moments we were on the verge of not going.

We figured the chances of winning were low and that it would take such a lot of effort to get us all up to London, especially with Trinity feeling unwell, that it might be best to give it a miss.

At the very last moment, we decided we would go and play it by ear – if Trinity's symptoms worsened we'd head home early – although the bakes had to be up there first thing, the judges' announcement wasn't due until 3pm.

We ended up having a really great day. Judging time came and everyone gathered around, with Eric Lanlard making the announcement. There were four winners and four runners-up to announce:

- Adult cakes category;
- Adult bakes category;
- Junior cakes category; and
- Junior bakes category.

Eric Lanlard rattled through all the announcements until he came to what we all thought was the end. For a second, we felt disheartened as Daniel's name hadn't been mentioned at all. Then someone pointed out that he hadn't announced the 'Junior Bakes' winner.

Eric looked at his papers a second time to check who had been missed and read out Daniel's name as the winner. We couldn't believe it.

The prize was to meet Mary Berry that very day for afternoon tea at 5pm. Daniel also won himself a gorgeous bright yellow Kenwood KMix stand-mixer and a signed copy of one of Mary Berry's cookbooks.

I was ridiculously excited to be Daniel's 'plus one' for the afternoon tea – and incredibly annoyed at myself for not having bothered to do my hair or make-up, having rushed out the house that morning!

The winners of each category and their plus-ones sat around the table and then she arrived. She sat at the head of the table, with Daniel on the long edge closest to her and me next to Daniel – just one seat away from Mary Berry! I couldn't help getting my phone out and taking photos for Instagram (and then reading in a media article afterwards that she doesn't like phones at the table – oops!).

We were all speechless. It truly felt like meeting the actual Queen because we all felt unable to speak. She politely asked a couple of questions to the winners. The whole experience was completely surreal – if you had told me at any point before in my entire life that I would one day be having afternoon tea with Mary Berry, I would never have believed it. Yet with this amazing hobby, it happened!

CHAPTER 8

When comping costs more

Comping is a great hobby when finances are tight as it's a way of enjoying all manner of things that are otherwise outside your budget. At the same time, however, some prizes do still come at a price.

As I mentioned in Chapter 6, I prefer not to pay to enter competitions. I avoid buying lottery tickets, I won't pay for premium texts or phone calls, and I'm even reluctant to buy stamps for postal comps now that postage costs are so high. However, while paying a modest fee to enter a competition is one thing, paying a premium to enjoy a prize is quite another. A prize may seem wonderful at first glance, but I strongly recommend checking whether there are any extra costs involved before accepting it!

For us, most London-based prizes end up incurring travel costs, which although not massive during off-peak hours, can still add up considerably over time. So, for each of the Movember meals I mentioned back in Chapter 3, for example, we had to get ourselves to London. I've also won cinema tickets in London, but by the time I'd paid for the train, it would probably have been cheaper just to buy tickets in my local cinema! Of course, if you can get enough prizes to combine them all for one big day out, your travel costs work out much lower, while your day is jam-packed with even more excitement!

52 Sleeps with Laterooms.com

A prime example of paying to enjoy a prize was the wonderful 52 Sleeps prize we won with Laterooms.com. The prize value was officially £10,000, and comprised a one-night break at 52 locations across the UK. However, with locations as far flung as Scotland (we live in south-east England), the reality of being able to take the entire prize was slim. In addition, no travel costs were covered, so that had to be factored in to our own budget.

Many of the places were geared up for couples rather than families which left us with another dilemma – how would a family of five be able to take this prize?

57

Thankfully, the Laterooms.com team were brilliant and although we got nowhere near the 52 nights, thanks to their help making all the booking arrangements, we managed to have a two-week break in the form of a UK road trip. To accommodate the five of us, Laterooms.com booked us a pair of rooms where they could, and where that wasn't possible, the five of us bunked up together. We didn't make it as far as Scotland, but we did get to Liverpool and Leeds, which are pretty far from our usual UK breaks.

But what about the extra costs? Well, in addition to the travelling costs, a lot of the actual venues were quite isolated and away from city centres or shopping facilities. With most of them having no self-catering facilities, dining out every night added a massive extra cost.

Nevertheless, it was a wonderful prize and we enjoyed ourselves thoroughly. We made many happy memories on that trip and have nothing but love for the people at Laterooms.com who helped make it all happen.

Dining at Noma

This was another incredible prize, but because I was breastfeeding at the time, I had to take my baby with us, along with Granny to look after her while we were actually taking the prize meal. This meant flying the whole family out to Copenhagen as there would have been no-one left to look after the boys at home.

So, we ended up with the additional costs of flights, accommodation and food for four extra people! Again, it was totally worth it for the experience, but I recognise that we were lucky to be able to afford to do this, as there have undoubtedly been times in our lives that we wouldn't have been able to justify such extra costs.

Staying at the Royal Garden Hotel

When we won the incredible prize of a night's stay at the luxurious Royal Garden Hotel in London via a Twitter party with Tots100 and E-cloth, we were over the moon.

The people arranging our booking were just amazing and the staff at the hotel really went to great lengths to make us feel welcome.

We had a fabulous stay and they even upgraded our room to a bigger one (given that most London hotel rooms are pretty small, the upgrade was especially welcome). Whilst breakfast was included in our stay, our evening dinner was not, so we ended up spending the equivalent of a week's grocery shopping on one meal at the Royal Garden Hotel. Of course, we didn't have to eat there, but after a long day in London it made sense to do so and it helped get the most out of the experience of staying there.

CHAPTER 9

Close but no cigar

Sometimes when people hear about my hobby, they think it's easy or that I'm just a mega-lucky person where good things happen to me all the time. In fact, it often feels far from it – whether it's health issues for myself and my family, putting my foot in it by doing or saying the wrong thing, or literally, by treading in dog poo – it's amazing just how much bad luck seems to come my way!

If you're reading this and thinking that winning all these prizes has been easy then think again! It *is* possible – I've done it – but it isn't easy. It takes time – a lot of time. In fact, the amount of time and effort that you put in certainly does affect the number of wins you're likely to have. There are ways of being strategic to improve the odds as I've mentioned, but if you want to see results, you've got to commit the time and effort to doing it.

Something that also needs to be mentioned is that *before* I started to win lots of prizes, I experienced *many* occasions where I *didn't* win prizes. I was runner-up, often in competitions without runner-up prizes, or I would come second place with a naff prize compared to the main prize.

Instead of giving up, however, I was encouraged by the fact that I was getting closer. I was learning the kinds of things that stand out. I was learning what promoters are looking for and I kept trying. I kept tweaking my entries and trying different things until the wins did start coming in.

A great example of one of my near wins came from a children's competition with a kids' yoghurt brand, which ran alongside the release of the latest Ice Age film. The kids made an awesome collage based on Ice Age and we sent it in. The first prize was a skiing holiday. We didn't win but we got sent a runner-up prize of Ice Age goodies – a Tupperware style lunchbox, a drawstring bag and a couple of other bits and pieces. It might have been nothing to write home about but the kids still liked it.

Considering the amount of effort the boys put into their entry, it would be easy to feel disappointed and, sure, there was a sense of 'what if' as we were so close. But instead of dwelling on the fact that we hadn't won, I was actually excited by how close we had come.

Dealing with disappointment remains a work in progress for me. If I've pulled out all the stops for a competition and I don't win, then I still get a low feeling in the pit of my stomach. The closest I can compare this to is going for an interview for a job you really, really want and then the rejection letter arrives in the post.

I don't think the feeling was as strong in the very early days of comping because obviously there are no guarantees with this hobby. So I'd get my entry in, wish, wait and hope, but there was no expectation. If a win did come then it was a genuine surprise filled with excitement and joy.

But the double-edged sword of this hobby is that as you get better at it, learning the tricks of what makes a stand-out entry, and start to get some wins under your belt, a sense of expectation creeps in. When you've put in heaps of effort and you sense it is good enough to be a winning entry, there follows the crash of disappointment when the winners are announced and you find you're not among them.

I've adopted four strategies to help me with this:

- *Don't invest too much emotional energy into an entry.* I do my best. Sometimes it can take a long time to prepare an entry – particularly for video competitions, recipe competitions or posing with props to get a photo just right. But if I lose my sense of expectation when I enter it, then I find I'm not so upset with the outcome. I know not everyone would agree with this and it tends to go against a 'positive thinking' mentality but I see it as letting go and letting the best man (or woman) win.

- *Learn from the winning entry.* Particularly at the start of my comping journey, I found it really useful to take the time to look at the winning entries and get a feel for why they stood out to the judges. I do my best not to copy someone else's idea too closely by replicating it for a future competition, but there is definitely inspiration to be had from the ideas in other people's entries. So, by using the opportunity to learn from someone else's winning entry, I have turned that sense of loss or disappointment into a positive outcome of learning for the future.

- *Celebrate the winner's success.* Don't post negative comments unless you have a genuine reason to suspect foul play. If I get the chance, I'll add a 'congratulations' comment on a social media post – because I know how nice it is when others congratulate me on a win. I'll remind myself of how the winner will be jumping for joy at their win and that helps me feel pleased for them – even more so if it is one of my comping friends.

- *Remind yourself that there is always next time.* Many promoters and brands run regular competitions week in, week out, month in, month out or sometimes year in, year out. If you don't win, just remember there is always next time (and the prize may be even better!).

CHAPTER 10

A win a day takes the pleasure away

It's easy to be downbeat when you're not winning, but would you believe the same can hold true when you *are* winning?

This chapter was always going to be the hardest to write. So far, I've put it off for a year, during which time I've discovered that I am a great procrastinator. A brilliant procrastinator in fact. I can muster up the energy and enthusiasm to do practically any task if it gets me out of getting to the nitty gritty of this chapter. In fact, just this morning, my bathroom needed a top-to-toe deep-clean and there was no way I could even make a start on this chapter until said cleaning was done. But now I'm out of excuses. The book is almost complete and I can avoid this no longer.

The truth is, this wonderful hobby has given me and my family the most unique and wonderful of experiences. It's given us lifelong memories to treasure. It's helped my kids enjoy fabulous Christmases and birthdays and holidays when times have been financially tough. It's a hobby I recommend to everyone I know.

And yet, it's also given me the darkest of times. Rewind to the summer of my first year of comping … By then I was in the flow. I'd learned to recognise what a winning entry looked like and combined with the oodles of time I was spending on Facebook, stuck at home with a new baby, the wins were coming in thick and fast.

The August of that year, the winning e-mails and notifications were pinging in pretty much daily, and yet I have never been unhappier in my life. It wasn't the comping that caused it, but it wasn't helping. My only source of joy and happiness during that time would come in the few moments after a winning e-mail landed in my inbox.

The rest of the time I would cry. I would struggle through the day, longing for the kids to go to bed so I could turn my computer back on for more comping. I would skip showers and meals in order to squeeze in another handful of competitions.

Such was my fear of missing a single competition, I was spending anything from five to seven hours on Facebook every night. No matter how much anyone tried to reason with me and explain just how ridiculous it was that I was spending more hours doing this than I'd be spending in a full-time job, I just wouldn't listen.

The trigger was post-natal depression compounded by grief that I'd never dealt with. I did see a counsellor eventually, but I would sit there in my sessions feeling that I was missing out on comping time so it didn't really help.

I didn't feel that it could be dealt with as an 'addiction' as although I realised even at the time that it very much had become an addiction, I didn't feel it warranted the same level of help/treatment/care/understanding as someone with perhaps an alcohol or drug addiction. After all, this was supposed to be a fun hobby. I was winning loads of stuff. No-one could understand why I wasn't happy about that.

But it was indeed an addiction because I couldn't allow myself to go to bed until I'd spent hours scrolling through the last 24 hours of my Facebook newsfeed, followed by all the tabs I'd opened on my computer for the competitions I needed to enter that day. On top of this were the 'creative' or 'effort' comps, some of which would take hours in their own right. Looming deadlines *had* to be met and nothing could be ignored – after all, what if my entry would have been the winning one?

I was routinely staying awake until 3 or 4am, knowing full well that my baby would be awake and needing me at around 6am meaning that I would only get a couple of hours sleep at night. It was clearly crazy, but it took a long time for me to acknowledge that. No-one can cope for any length of time on just two or three hours of sleep a night, and yet I was putting myself through this day in day out, out of choice. Except it wasn't a choice – or at least it didn't feel like a choice at the time. Comping was my only escape from reality. Yes, in the same way that some people turn to drugs or alcohol as an escape, this was my way of escaping. Even now, I feel faintly ridiculous to put that in writing when drug and alcohol abuse can have such devastating consequences; and so again, I feel uncomfortable, even guilty about putting my 'problem' in anything like the same category. Perhaps gambling is a better parallel for understanding my addiction: I may not have been gambling away money, but I was gambling away so much of my time and my quality of life with my children.

It has been a long journey, but over the years I have managed to scale back my hobby until it no longer feels like an addiction but an enjoyable pastime that may be a big part of my life, but doesn't control my life.

During these years, I've grappled with a lot of feelings of guilt. There have been times when *any* time comping became associated with guilt. When I've gone cold turkey, I find that I miss it so much that I end up quite literally dreaming about comping – and trust me, waking up to discover you haven't had that big cash win or huge prize holiday that you've just been dreaming about is a pretty miserable way to start the day.

I've settled for spending less time on the comps, being far more selective about what I enter – remembering the joy the prize will give someone else who does really want or need it.

I get my joy and happiness from elsewhere – from spending time with my family. Of course, I still enjoy the little buzzes and bursts of joy that come from those wins, and as a family we love making memories by enjoying the prizes and experiences that we've won, but comping is no longer my sole source of happiness.

I've sought to understand the reasons why I enjoy competitions so much. It may surprise people to hear that I'm not an overly materialistic person – I have never felt the need to have the latest clothes or gadgets. And yet so often competitions give the impression of being about 'stuff' (as indeed they often are). These days, unless it's something I really need or foods that I really enjoy, I tend to enjoy winning experiences more than winning 'stuff'. The days out, the weird and wonderful activities and the holidays that give me precious memories with my family are some of the most special wins.

And it's not just the wins – it's the process. Being creative is an excellent method to express oneself and build self-esteem.

I'm not one for sob stories (don't get me started on people using them for competition entries!), but for various reasons stemming from my upbringing, I have never had a great sense of self-worth or value.

Even when I have been good at something, I've had major imposter syndrome, not believed in myself and doubted my ability. The isolation of being a stay-at-home parent for over a decade has further exacerbated this. For parents, there's no annual appraisal; there's no-one there to tell you when you've done a good job; and you rarely get any thanks. I did manage a little self-employed work during those years, but as any freelancer will tell you, the praise is thin on the ground, and no-one, but no-one, has your back. For someone with tons of self-confidence and self-belief that probably isn't an issue, but I used to love my annual appraisal at work when someone would take the time to remind me of all the things I'd done well that year.

For me, winning competitions gave me a sense of knowing that I'd 'got it right'. It was someone else judging my work and giving me a metaphorical pat on the back – something that I wasn't getting from any other area of my life.

The simple truth is that this hobby can be addictive. In fact, the more success you have as a comper, the more likely it is to become addictive. The feeling of winning is a walking-on-air, can't stop smiling, kind of feeling. And yet in the overall scheme of things, it's short-lived and superficial. Even with the big wins – the holidays, the incredible money-can't-buy experiences, and so on – the feeling doesn't last forever. Yes, it brings joy when there is good news. But the opposite is also true. When you've spent hours and hours or sometimes even days and days working on a competition entry, you can feel pretty low when you find out you haven't won, especially if your entry has been tailored for a specific brand so you won't even be able to 'recycle' it at some point in future.

CHAPTER 11

A hobby like any other?

It has taken a long time to escape the guilt that also became attached to this hobby as a result of my obsessive behaviour during that difficult time in my life. Although I've cut back on the amount of time and emotional investment I put into comping these days, if I start getting too enthusiastic, the guilt has a way of creeping back. Yet, if this was any other hobby – fishing, golf, stamp-collecting, baking – *any other hobby* – I can't imagine that I'd feel guilty about it. So what makes comping different?

Actually, I've found a number of things that make comping stand out from the more mainstream pastimes out there.

Comper-friendly or not?
One of the more curious things I've observed over the years is a degree of animosity towards compers, emanating from others within the game itself – sometimes this comes from brands, sometimes from bloggers running competitions, and sometimes from other compers themselves!

Anti-comper brands
Occasionally, I've seen terms and conditions that stipulate no 'professional' compers. This grates with me because I doubt there are many compers out there that would consider themselves 'professional' – it's a hobby not a career! Yes, some compers do sell their prizes to help make ends meet, but could they live off comping as a steady income? I very much doubt it.

Meanwhile, some brands run effort-based competitions where they promise to choose a winner based on the quality of their entry, yet in their efforts to pick a 'genuine customer' rather than a comper, end up selecting something mundane rather than anything exciting where the entrant has gone the extra mile.

This is frustrating because (a) if someone has bothered to go the extra mile in a judged competition then surely their creativity and effort should be celebrated, and (b) how and why are they differentiating between 'genuine customers' and 'compers'? I have lost count of the number of times that comping has introduced me to a brand and I have gone on to buy lots and lots from them, becoming a loyal customer in the process – regardless of whether I have won anything from them. Indeed, one of the fundamental aims of competitions is to raise brand awareness. I might not have rushed out to buy those products immediately, but when the time came, they were top of mind – I felt I 'knew' and 'trusted' those brands better thanks to my previous interaction with them. Which leads us to (c): there are plenty of ways to restrict competitions to 'genuine customers' only, the most obvious being 'purchase necessary' competitions. To be sure, opening up competitions to the wider public gets bigger numbers involved and lots more brand 'buzz'; however, any promoter that actively wants to prevent certain people from entering its competition really needs to give full consideration to exactly what it hopes to achieve by running a competition in the first place and ensure that it designs the competition in such a way as to get entries only from its target demographic.

Anti-comper bloggers
Again, this saddens me – especially as I am a blogger myself. Bloggers are often more vocal about their feelings – and rightly so – but one side effect of this is that there have been some quite heated debates about whether bloggers running competitions should allow compers to enter them. This has happened to such an extent that there is now a 'comper friendly' badge that bloggers can display on their blogs.

At this point I feel like screaming out – compers are just ordinary people – often perfectly nice, wonderful, lovely people, who simply enjoy entering competitions.

Sometimes they come across this hobby from a place of despair and it offers them a little glimmer of hope – perhaps it helps them to connect with others and find a sense of community. Just as blogging offers a community of like-minded individuals and supportive friendships, comping is simply another hobby that can also help people.

I sympathise with bloggers wanting to ring-fence their competitions for their 'genuine readers'. Nevertheless, there are non-confrontational ways of doing this, such as not promoting the competition beyond the blog itself. Rather than encouraging entrants to share it on social media they could simply introduce an element of effort – whether it be commenting about that blog's niche or getting entrants to engage by uploading their own photos related to the blog's content (such as a travel blogger asking for a travel related photo to be entered as an entry into a competition).

Finally, a point for bloggers to remember is that competitions are a great way to attract new, regular readers – I have certainly found many new blogs in this way!

Anti-comper compers

Now this does sound like an oxymoron if ever there was one, but amazingly, there is a small subset of compers who don't like the fact that there are other compers out there! They moan about how much harder it is to win these days because there are more compers, and they moan that the same people keep winning the prizes.

I have to admit that when I first began this hobby in earnest, I would get frustrated when I found a low-entry competition and planned a good entry for it, only for the comp to get picked up by one or more of the competition-sharing sites and, all of a sudden, loads of entries would come flooding in, thus reducing my own chances.

I would also see the same few names coming up time and time again as winners. I'd feel a little envious, but if I took a step back and looked at it logically, it was usually people who spent a lot of time entering competitions, who had put a lot of effort into their entries, and if I was honest, they were good entries and well deserving of a win.

In my early days of comping, I remember people saying that 'there are plenty of competitions to go around'. That too annoyed me at first, as I figured that if everyone was trying to enter the same competitions, then surely the odds would worsen. As I write this six years later, however, I know for sure that there are more competitions out there than I could possibly dream of entering, even if I spent every moment of my day glued to my computer, finding and entering competitions.

These days, I even struggle to find the time to enter ones that I really want to. On top of this, I'm far more selective about the things I do enter, often asking myself the 'do I really want it or need it' question first.

The other side of the coin is that there are also plenty of compers who *do* believe in sharing, who give each other great encouragement and inspiration, who celebrate each other's successes, who tag each other in competitions that may be of interest, and who simply enjoy chatting about this niche hobby in a world where none of their offline friends 'get' what it's all about. I genuinely feel happy when my comping friends win a competition – even if it is a competition that I was hoping to win myself.

There is a lesson for us all in the whole anti-comper/comper-friendly debate – it shines a light on how judgemental we can all be. I include myself in this as I know that despite my best efforts not to, it is all too easy to jump to conclusions about other people, based on no more than their looks, their mannerisms, their beliefs, their preferences or whatever.

I've made many friends through comping, and if I've learned one thing from this, it's that there is often more than meets the eye. Behind the scenes, people are often battling with their own health, their family's health or circumstances, tragedies, difficulties, dilemmas; and comping offers an escape much like any other hobby would.

Being polite/saying thank you

It's possible that some of the anti-comper sentiment comes from the few that spoil it for the many. I always always always make a point of saying thank you when I have won a prize – however big or small it may be. In my response to the notification I sound grateful and pleased, and when the prize arrives, I try to snap a photo and thank the promoter either via social media or by e-mail. It only takes a moment to do, it reassures them that the prize has arrived, and gratitude costs nothing.

I hear of stories (and have occasionally experienced myself when I have run competitions on my own blog) of people replying with their address details without a single thank you or nicety. Sometimes there is no acknowledgment or thank you of the prize arriving, which can leave the promoter worried or confused because the prize may well have been sent out by a different company or may have got lost in the post.

In short, it really is worth taking a moment to say thanks.

Comparison is the thief of joy

Have you ever heard the phrase 'comparison is the thief of joy'? It can apply to so many areas of life – when we compare our jobs with others, or perhaps we envy other families with seemingly better-behaved children. In the online world, the pressure can be even stronger when we look at Pinterest-perfect photos and neat Instagram squares of curated bliss.

But do these pictures tell a true story? How often have you seen your friends' smiley holiday photos on Facebook but when you next see them in the flesh, they tell you that the whole break was a complete disaster?!

During my comping years, there have been plenty of times when I have found myself envying other people's prize hauls. I've felt massive pangs of disappointment and jealousy all rolled into one when someone else has won a prize that I'd been longing for.

Left unchecked, I know this would have left me feeling bitterness and resentment, so I'm very careful to watch those inner feelings if they start to show negativity.

Nowadays, I love hearing about other people's prize wins – not so I can wish it had been me, nor to be inspired or motivated to try harder, but because I feel genuinely pleased for them.

I know they would have experienced that same feeling of elation and joy that I've experienced when I have won a prize and I feel happy for them to have experienced that.

Even when someone seems to be winning *all* the prizes (which can't be true, as there really are enough prizes to go around!) I can still feel happy for them because I know that they will have been pouring in hours of effort behind the scenes to achieve those results. Those wins are well deserved – it's hard work paying off.

I've been fortunate not to have experienced too much hostility myself, but I have seen how bitter and nasty some people can get over what is meant to be a fun hobby. Unless there has been foul play or cheating, I can't see the point of negativity. There are times we all have to accept that even though we may not necessarily agree with what has been chosen as the winning entry, the judges' choice is the judges' choice. End of.

So, to enjoy this hobby at its best, see it collaboratively rather than selfishly. Help out other compers – if you spot a prize that you know they would love to win – tag them. Don't compare your prize wins with other people's. Someone may have won a prize worth thousands, but you may win something small that you've always wanted. Or you may scoop something that money can't buy because it is so special and unique that it really does have no monetary value – how do you compare that?

Be happy with what you do and don't worry about others judging you – that's their problem. Spend the amount of time and effort that suits you – again, there's no point comparing it with what someone else does. You may be juggling a full-time job with your hobby, or you may have your hands full with a new baby, or you may have a disability that prevents you from posing for photos while doing extreme sports.

Spend only the amount of money that suits you. While I personally avoid pay-to-enter competitions, that doesn't make them wrong. While I might buy an extra pack or two of my usual brand for a purchase-necessary competition, some people stockpile products in order to maximise their chances of winning. Some people buy props for their creative competitions, other people just improvise. One man's meat is another man's poison!

The important thing is to know your budget, stick to the time you have available, and comp only when the mood suits.

CHAPTER 12

Everything but the kitchen sink

Whilst this hobby can take a lot of time, dedication and commitment to see the results, I do feel 'lucky' and blessed to have won so many things that I have really wanted or needed at any particular time. Of course, things don't always work that way, as I've never managed to win a new mobile phone or new microwave, despite needing one for years, but in general I feel very fortunate.

As I've mentioned, I've enjoyed some amazing experiences thanks to comping. Meeting Mary Berry was of course a dream come true, but I've also done things I would never have dreamed of. Thanks to Laterooms.com, I've stayed on a boat decked out as the Joker's Lair (as in from the Batman film!) and a lighthouse with a TARDIS on the roof and a Dalek inside it.

Comping has also helped to reduce my weekly shopping bills, thanks to winning household products such as cleaning detergents, as well as vouchers to spend at various supermarkets, and I've been able to replace old baking tins with brand-new shiny ones. It has also helped avoid big-ticket purchases, such as Trinity's baby stroller or a new stand mixer for the kitchen.

Indeed, some of the best prizes have come in the form of timely solutions. For example, when we had some building work done on our house, we ended up running out of budget to renew the front door, which was in desperate need of replacing. So when I won a new front door, I was thrilled because it was exactly what we needed at the time!

Winning a door may sound pretty random, but over the years, I have seen many different competitions advertised with strange or extreme prizes. If you look hard enough, there are bungee jumps to be won, hotel stays in cranes and on ski lifts, and even entire kitchen or garden makeovers! You literally could win everything *including* a kitchen sink. But I haven't … yet!

When I first started comping, I would enter anything and everything I came across, regardless of what the prize was or whether I particularly wanted it.

Over the years, however, I've learned that wining tastes so much sweeter when the prize is something I really want or need, or if it is something I can gift to someone who will really appreciate it. This means I can share happiness without the stress of trying to sell unwanted items.

Indeed, these days, I take a moment to think – if I were to receive that winning e-mail, would my heart skip with delight or would the win make no odds to me? If the answer is the latter, then I don't enter; rather, I sit back and hope that someone who really wants or needs the prize will enjoy it instead.

In short, comping has changed my life. Some day I hope to cover the period between these early comping years (which I have written about in this book) and now in a new book, *The Happy Comper*, as there have been so many more magical and memorable experiences since.

AFTERWORD

Why Overcoming the Odds?

Whilst writing this book, I used the working title of *'The woman who won things'* – the reason being that one of my favourite children's authors, Allan Ahlberg, has a book by the same name which I had bought for my children several years ago. I had hoped that Ahlberg's book would have been more about winning things. From memory, other than reference to it early on, the book quickly moves onto a different storyline and doesn't turn out to be about comping or winning after all. Feeling disappointed (I know it was only a children's story book but still I had built up my level of excitement in anticipation of reading it), *my* book was definitely going to be about a woman who won things with lots of stories of comping and prizes and winning in it.

But as the book drew to a close, I couldn't help but feel that the title of *'The woman who won things'* didn't paint the whole picture. So, I changed the title. The title of *'Overcoming the Odds'* reflects both the essence of what it takes to win competitions (by overcoming the odds, whether you win a prize drawn at random or have put in the effort with a creative endeavour which results in a win) as well as a glimpse into the backdrop against which this book was written.

This book has taken an age to write in snatched pockets of time, then edited with the help of an amazing friend who I will forever be indebted to, and it has been written in the midst of chaos and turmoil at home.

Any parent of a child with a chronic illness will be familiar with the constant treadmill of hospital appointments, tests, scans, therapies and treatments. In between those commitments there are the days spent on the phone arranging said appointments and chasing the results from said tests, scans, therapies and treatments. In addition, you are looking after the child concerned on a day-to-day basis with all the challenges that presents – in Trinity's case, picking up a simple common childhood illness like a cold can land her in hospital. Chicken pox meant a week-long hospital stay on a drip! Throw into the mix another child diagnosed with Asperger's, plus another thought to be on the autistic spectrum but not yet diagnosed and I can see why people have always said to me that I have my hands full.

And as if that wasn't enough, I myself had a total hip replacement operation at the (relatively young) age of 40 and despite everything else going on in my life, I have to confess that psychologically and emotionally that was one of the toughest things I have been through.

I am not one for pity-parties and I only mention all these things because I know everyone has their own battles. They may not come in the same shape or form as my battles but they are very real and just as significant in their lives.

The focus of this book, my hobby of entering competitions, has been a lifeline, a distraction, an escape at times when I've most needed it. It has also brought me valuable friendships that have helped me get through the toughest days. It has brought hope and excitement at times when our family have needed it most.

So, in writing this book, I hope that whatever the odds you are up against, it will offer a glimpse of hope that you don't have to accept things as they are and that you can take control of one area of your life and do something to help bring about some good experiences and create happy memories by *Overcoming the Odds*.

ABOUT THE AUTHOR

Rebecca Beesley has earned her title of 'Comper' by entering thousands of competitions over many years. Alongside her hobby, she is a mother to three rapidly-growing children and wife to Richard. She is passionate about raising awareness that arthritis is not just an 'old persons' disease but that young children and even babies can and do get this horrible autoimmune condition, and is a strong supporter of the Juvenile Arthritis Research project (www.jarproject.org).

She enjoys baking in her spare time (although she claims to have more baking disasters than successes), and runs the popular and successful family blog called The Beesley Buzz. You can follow her adventures at https://thebeesleybuzz.blogspot.co.uk.

Printed in Great Britain
by Amazon